Block Play

The Complete Guide to
Learning and Playing with Blocks

Sharon MacDonald

Illustrations: Katheryn Davis

Dedication

To my mother, Margaret Love Gary (1916-1999),
whose four daughters, Gloria, Shula, Dawn, and Sharon
were the building blocks of her life.

Block play

The Complete Guide
to Learning and
Playing with
Blocks

Sharon MacDonald

Published by Gryphon House, Inc.
10726 Tucker Street, Beltsville Md 20705
Visit us on the web at www.gryphonhouse.com

Library of Congress Cataloging-in-Publication Data

MacDonald, Sharon, 1942–
    Block play : the complete guide to learning and playing with blocks / Sharon MacDonald ; illustrations, Katheryn Davis.
        p. cm.
    Includes bibliographical references (p.) and index.
    ISBN 0-87659-253-1
    1. Blocks (Toys) 2. Block building (Children's activity) 3. Educational games. 4. Early childhood education —Activity programs. I. Title: Complete guide to learning and playing with blocks. II. Title.

    GV1218.B6M M33 2001
    790.1'33—dc21
                                                            2001023136

Illustrations: Katheryn Davis
Cover photograph: Straight Shots Product Photography, Ellicott City, Maryland.

Bulk purchase

Gryphon House books are available at special discount when purchased in bulk for special premiums and sales promotions as well as for fund-raising use. Special editions or book excerpts also can be created to specification. For details, contact the Director of Sales at the address above.

Disclaimer

The publisher and the authors cannot be held responsible for injury, mishap, or damages incurred during the use of or because of the activities in this book. The author recommends appropriate and reasonable supervision at all times based on the age and capability of each child.

Table of Contents

Chapter 5—Involving Parents (Or Taking Blocks Home) 43

Chapter 6—Using Other Construction Materials (Or Stacking Up Alternatives) 55

Chapter 7—Making Connections to New Learning (Or Block Tracks) 63

Unit Block Activities

Beginning Activities 72

Intermediate Activities   99

Advanced Activities   121

Activities Using Other Construction Materials

Introduction

(Or Learning Begins With Building Blocks)

This is a book about blocks, and what children can learn from building with them.

It is also a book about Robert, a young child who loved playing in the Block Center. Robert felt comfortable in the Block Center because his "friends and family" were there. (Well, not exactly, but we are getting ahead of ourselves.) The point is that Robert learned most of what he needed to know to be successful in school by playing in the Block Center. It was his favorite place when he was in my class in San Antonio, Texas.

Almost every class has a Robert, a child who has a hard time making the transition from home to school. During the first two weeks of school, Robert cried every morning when his mother left. To help Robert and the other children adjust to school, I asked each child to bring in a photograph of their family or friends. I made a "Friends and Family Bulletin Board" (or "F and F Board"), and the children hung their photos on it. Whenever a child felt lonesome for home, I would suggest that he or she look at the "F and F Board" for a while.

Robert brought in a photo of his family lined up on the front steps of his massive, two-story home. Other children brought in photos of their families inside their house, some eating dinner or blowing out birthday candles.

Robert visited his photo often.

After a few weeks, we needed the "F and F Board" for other things. The children were comfortable with the classroom by then—it had become part of their lives. We said good-bye to the photos of our friends and families, except for Robert. He was not yet ready to let go, so I found a spot for his photograph on a wall in the Block Center.

Although I did not realize it at the time, by choosing the Block Center wall for Robert's photograph, I had chosen Robert's center-of-play. When I passed out the center tags to the children each day, Robert always put his name in the Block Center, so he could be close to his "home and family." Robert played there day after day, raking the blocks off the shelves, stacking them up, and spreading them out on the floor. He worked next to the other children, but not with them—in parallel play.

Soon, I realized that Robert was not selecting other centers in the classroom. He would move to another center if I asked him to, but he was most comfortable in the Block Center. I became concerned. I wondered if he would be able to learn what he needed to be successful in school by playing only in the Block Center.

I decided to research the topic before deciding what to do. I read *The Block Book* by Hirsch (ed.) and *The Complete Block Book* by Provenzo (contributor) and Brett. I also read some helpful articles: "Block Construction" by Reifel in *Young Children,* November, 1984; "What Block Play Can Do for Children" by Brown and Briggs in *Texas Child Care Quarterly,* Spring, 1988; and, "Blocks Are Not (circle all): Messy, Expensive, Difficult" by Karges-Bone in *Dimensions,* Fall, 1991. These books and articles reassured me that blocks are a tool I could use to teach all of the skills and concepts necessary for children to be successful learners. Blocks work for all children—not just Robert. I was delighted with what I found!

I learned that free play with blocks provides children with opportunities to develop many skills and concepts. Playing with blocks helps children learn in ways that are best suited to them. Blocks provide children with opportunities to be successful with the skills they have. To help children progress, observe what they do in the Block Center. Then, it is simply a matter of adding essential materials at the right time, a subject we will get into in detail later.

Children acquire skills such as sorting, matching, counting, sequencing, and learning shapes by playing with blocks. And in the process, they develop gross and fine motor skills. Through block play, children also observe physical properties, such as how force affects objects, and how structures react to force. The knowledge that children acquire is extended to other aspects of their lives. For example, they learn that unstable things fall down while stable things do not. Children learn that blocks have individual and group characteristics that are interrelated in complicated ways. By playing with blocks, children are acquiring the skills they need to be successful.

Why Build with Blocks?

Chapter 1

(Or How Blocks Stack Up)

Why build with blocks? Good question! After all, with so many other things to do at school, why should children stack blocks and push them around on the floor? What do children learn, anyway?

Through block play, children can learn to read, write, speak, and listen. Block play can teach them about math, science, and social studies. Block play often involves cooperative, collaborative learning, which helps children grow emotionally and socially. Block play also enhances their physical growth and development.

The early childhood curriculum topics and skills that children learn through block play are shown collectively in the illustrations on the following pages.

> See the **Math** in the unit blocks.
>
> See the **Science** in the y-switch block.
>
> See the **Art** in the constructions with cylinders.
>
> See the **Literacy** and **Language Arts** in the unit blocks.
>
> See the **Physical Development** in the bridge construction.
>
> See the **Social Studies** in the unit blocks.
>
> See the **Social and Emotional Growth** in the L-shaped construction.

The List of Block Center Skills (page 12) is a compilation of the illustrations on pages 13-19. It lists the skills that most children learn while playing with blocks. Post the list on one of the walls in the Block Center. It will remind you of the skills children are learning, and it will remind other people, such as parents and administrators, about the numerous opportunities children have to learn by playing with blocks.

What Children Learn Through Block Play

Children learn to

Use oral language in a variety of situations

Explore cause and effect

Represent a thought or an idea

Develop problem solving techniques

Form creative and critical thinking skills

Match objects in one-to-one correspondence

Use social skills appropriate to group behavior

Express quantities

Use language to establish and maintain relationships in the social structure

Demonstrate an understanding of parts and whole

Use vocabulary to compare same and different objects

Form data sets, or groups, by sorting and matching objects according to their attributes

Understand the consequences of social interaction

Acquire non-locomotor movement skills

Create, repeat, and extend patterns

Develop eye-hand coordination

Observe and follow safety rules

Put things in order using specific criteria

Understand mapping skills

Use the physical representations of addition and subtraction

Develop classification skills

Differentiate between sizes and shapes

Understand object relationships and recognition

Discuss how people help each other

Express and explore relative size

Understand gravity, stability, weight, and balance

Think creatively to make and implement plans

Realize the properties of matter

Discover the names and functions of buildings

Develop respect for the work of others

Make decisions and choices

Take reasonable risks to further their own learning and to broaden their interpersonal world

Let's talk about how to set up the Block Center!

Mathematics

- space
- shapes
- size
- order
- number
- fractions
- weight

- counting
- patterns
- equal/ unequal
- recognize sets or groups
- shortest/ longest
- tallest/ shortest
- estimate

- length
- depth
- width
- height
- mapping
- symmetry
- quantity

- similarities and differences
- classification
- planning
- measurement — volume, area
- graphing
- one-to-one correspondence
- part and whole relationships

13

Science

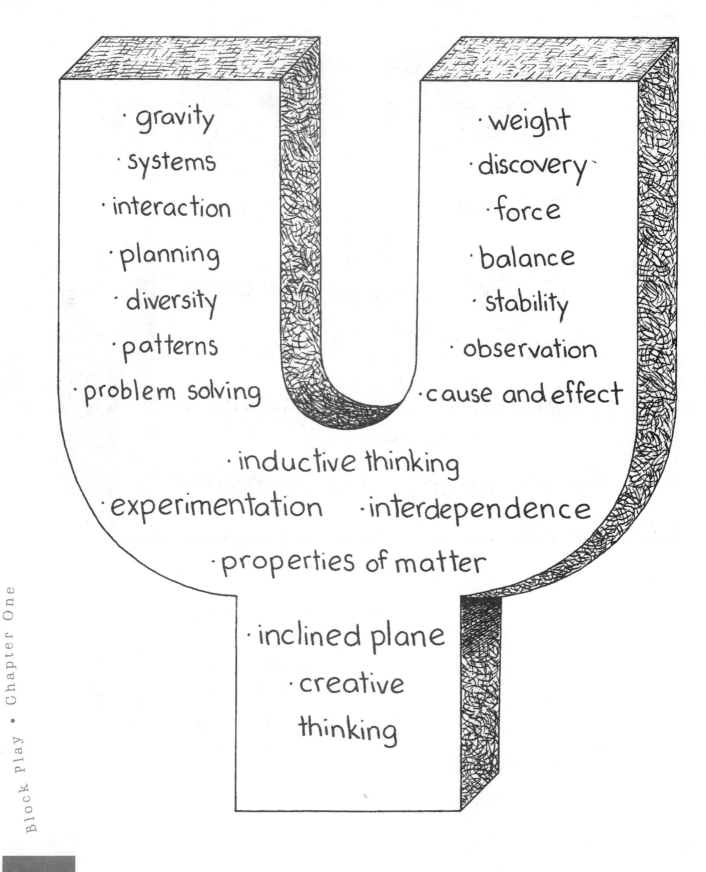

- gravity
- systems
- interaction
- planning
- diversity
- patterns
- problem solving
- weight
- discovery
- force
- balance
- stability
- observation
- cause and effect
- inductive thinking
- experimentation
- interdependence
- properties of matter
- inclined plane
- creative thinking

Art

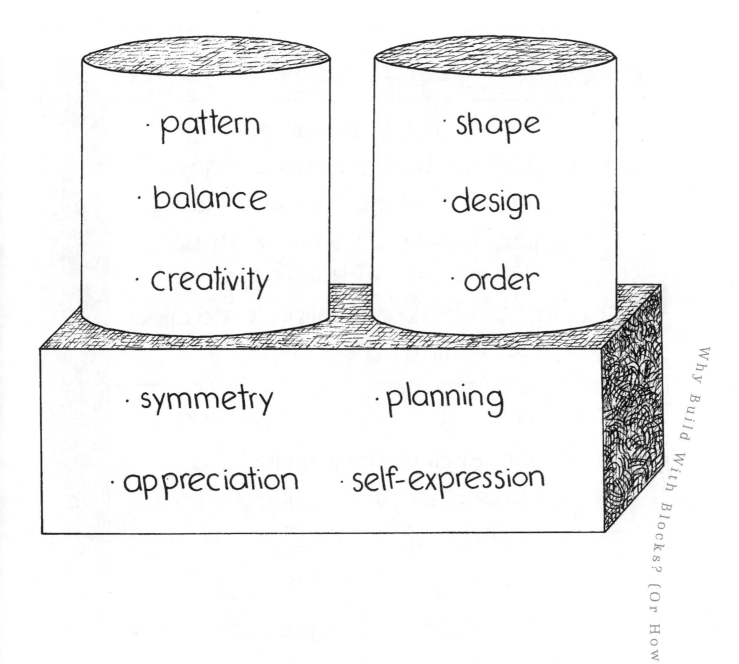

- pattern
- balance
- creativity

- shape
- design
- order

- symmetry
- appreciation

- planning
- self-expression

Literacy

· planning of building
· "reading" picture directions, signs
· discussion about functions of buildings
· naming, labeling, and making up
  stories about buildings
· exchange of ideas – sampling, predicting,
  confirming, integrating

· oral language   · rhyming
· understanding story sequence
· developing vocabulary
· clean-up directions
· building a sight word vocabulary
· using representations of objects and ideas

Physical Development

small muscles:

· visual perception   · finger control

· eye-hand coordination

· controlled hand manipulation

large muscles:	· body awareness
· sides of body working together	·squatting
· bending	
· moving through space	· balance

Social Studies

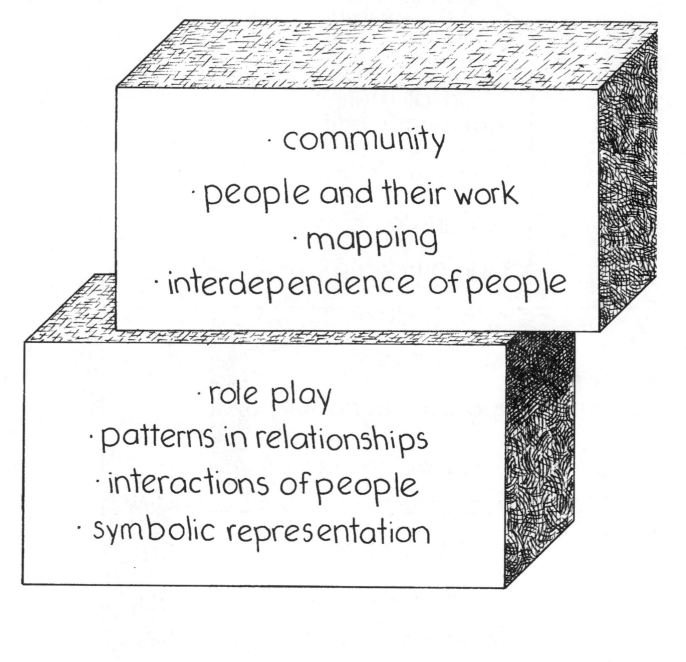

· community
· people and their work
· mapping
· interdependence of people

· role play
· patterns in relationships
· interactions of people
· symbolic representation

Social-Emotional

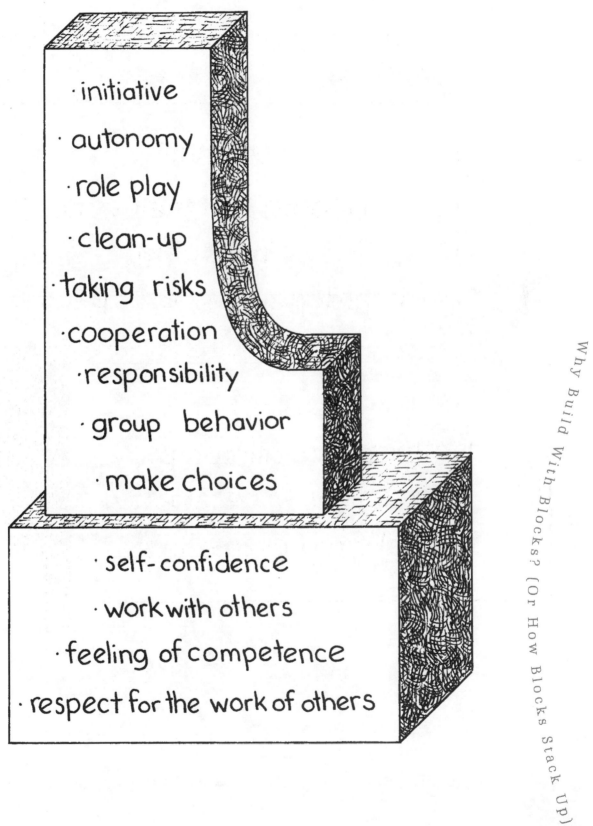

- initiative
- autonomy
- role play
- clean-up
- taking risks
- cooperation
- responsibility
- group behavior
- make choices

- self-confidence
- work with others
- feeling of competence
- respect for the work of others

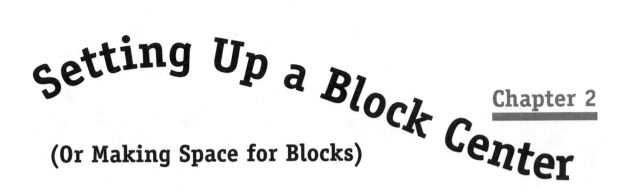

Setting Up a Block Center

(Or Making Space for Blocks)

Chapter 2

In the Introduction of this book, I introduced you to Robert. He spent most of his time in the Block Center because he liked being near the photo of his family. By working with the blocks and the accessories in the Block Center, Robert learned most of the skills and concepts he needed to learn.

When Robert first arrived in the classroom, I did not know it was possible to learn so much in one place. I did not want to move Robert to a new area just to teach him something else, so I read as much as I could about what children can learn in a well-designed block center. I discovered things I could do, such as adding the right accessories, to broaden Robert's learning.

Center Location and Arrangement

Where in the classroom do you put the Block Center? I chose one corner of the room, but other choices might make more sense for you (see illustration on page 22).

I placed a low-napped rug on the floor to define the space and reduce the noise from falling blocks. I stored the blocks in two open shelves—one against the wall and the other at the rug's edge to establish the boundary between the Block and Music Centers. Two feet

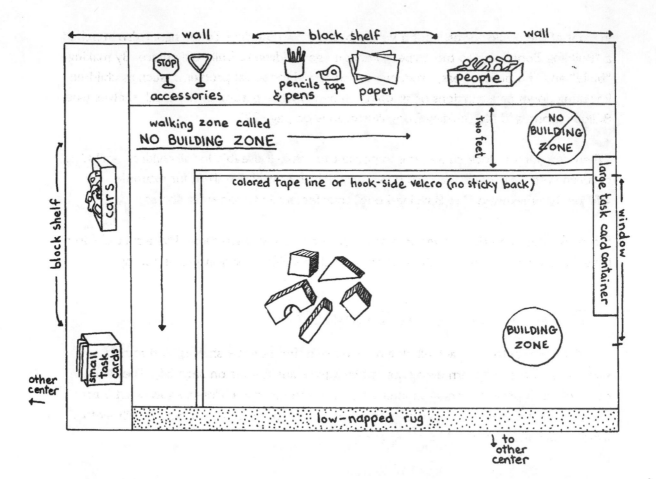

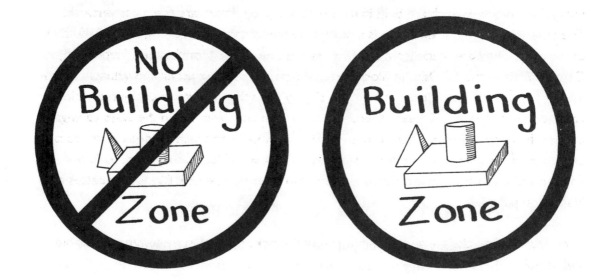

in front of the bookshelves, I put a Velcro-backed "No Building Zone" sign. I also attached a "Building Zone" sign to the carpet to encourage children to build only there. By making "build" and "no build" areas, I reduced the potential for social problems, such as children knocking down constructions or stepping on hands while getting to the block shelves (see Building Zone and No Building Zone illustrations on page 22).

When designing a block center, it is important to make it useable for all children, including children with disabilities. If a child is in a wheelchair or uses a walker, for example, you will need to make the "No Building Zone" four feet wide to allow for access.

Store the blocks on the shelves so that children can easily reach them. Make sure children have "to and from" access to the shelves as block-building activity increases nearby.

How to Use Block Silhouettes

Make silhouettes of each block type and place them on the shelves so that children will know where to return each type of block (see illustrations on page 24). The silhouettes will help prevent confusion at clean-up time and let the children know what blocks are available for building. If a visually impaired child is in the class, cut out the silhouettes from sandpaper so the child can feel them.

What Kind of Blocks to Buy

Before purchasing blocks, consider the age and number of the children in the classroom. Unit blocks, which are built in mathematical proportion, are the most versatile. The base unit block, for example, is a quadruple block; the others are ⅛, ¼, or ½ the size of the base. They are made from solid hardwood and will last for decades. Invented by Carolyn Pratt in the 1800s, unit blocks are still among the most useful and valuable equipment you can offer to children. It is interesting to note that in spite of all the technology created over the past 150 years, there has been little improvement in the ways to engage and teach young children. There is nothing like unit blocks to teach children math, vocabulary, and other skills. For example, as children work with blocks, they want to know what to call them and are motivated to learn their names (see Unit Block Silhouettes and Names on page 24).

Other kinds of blocks are also available, but unit blocks are the most common, durable, and useful.

The Type of Blocks by Age Group

The best blocks for children age two and under are foam, cardboard, paper bag, or cloth blocks; extra large Lego blocks; or large, hollow, wooden blocks. Three- and four-

Unit Block Silhouettes and Names

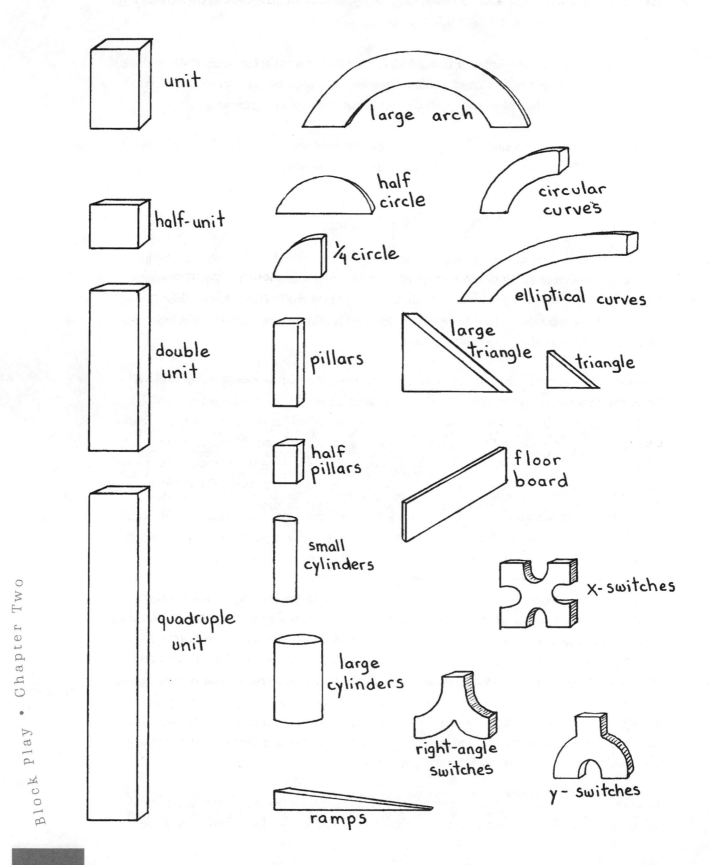

unit

large arch

half circle

circular curves

half-unit

¼ circle

elliptical curves

double unit

pillars

large triangle

triangle

half pillars

floor board

small cylinders

x-switches

quadruple unit

large cylinders

right-angle switches

y-switches

ramps

year-olds can use unit blocks, colored-cube blocks, parquetry blocks, Bristle Blocks, and large, hollow, wooden blocks with lots of accessories. Five- and six-year-olds can use the more unusually shaped unit blocks, tabletop blocks, Lincoln Logs, and Cuisenaire Rods. (See Chapter 6 for information on other building materials and the best ages to use them.)

NOTE ABOUT CARING FOR UNIT BLOCKS

Rub blocks liberally with mineral oil and a soft cloth. Let the mineral oil soak into the wood. When the oil has been absorbed, briskly rub the blocks with a soft, dry cloth. Do this about every two years.

How Many Blocks

Making sure there are enough blocks is very important. Generally, the number of blocks to have depends on the number of children in the center at one time. If there are too few blocks in the center, there will not be enough to go around, which can cause disagreements among the children.

To figure out the best block-to-children ratio, consider the number of children who will be in the center at one time and their age. There are many resource books and articles that suggest what block-to-children ratio to use. Personally, I have found that more than four or five children in the Block Center at one time is too chaotic. Next, consider the age of the children. By factoring in the age of the children and limiting the number of children to four or five, a good rule of thumb is: 200 blocks for three-year-olds, 300 blocks for four-year-olds, and 400 blocks for five-year-olds and older children.

How to Store Blocks

To store blocks on shelves, start from the left-hand corner of the top shelf and stack to the right. Store the smallest blocks first. Move left to right across the shelves, increasing the block size until you have stacked the largest and heaviest blocks on the bottom. Keeping most of the weight on the bottom of the bookcase helps stabilize the unit and makes it safer. Children can remove and replace the blocks in a more orderly way, and the organized storage invites them to examine the size differences among the blocks. By seeing the pattern of seriated blocks daily, they will learn about patterns. Learning about patterns is useful and essential for learning all subjects, and young children enjoy making patterns when they understand what a pattern is.

Children will also have an easier time putting blocks away because they will understand what to do. I have often said to them (while holding various blocks), "This is small, so it

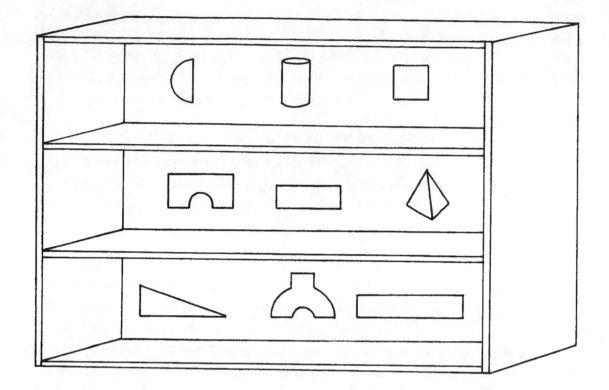

goes on the **top** shelf. This is large, so it goes on the **bottom**. Everyone needs to help at clean-up time." The children learn how to clean up and put the blocks **in order** on the shelves.

What Block Accessories to Use

I have often thought that block accessories are similar to "extras" that master chefs toss into their sauces to make a great meal taste like no other. The "extras" make all the difference in the taste. Block accessories are like that—they change the nature of the play. Accessories motivate children by adding new possibilities to their building. These additions invite different children into the action, piqued perhaps by the added accessory. Many children will simply be more curious about something new.

Accessories can be made from just about any material, including wood, plastic, or metal. They can be hard or flexible, real or make-believe. They can be people, animals, signs, and objects.

The best choices for purchased or constructed accessories are figures of people representing different racial and ethnic backgrounds and lifestyles. By choosing these accessories, children learn about each other. These accessories invite them to consider and appreciate the similarities and differences in themselves and others. It is best to use stand-up figures portraying non-sexist life roles. Make plenty of extended family members available so children can create the many different textures, roles, and configurations of families—the diversity that enriches our culture.

What other things can you use? Try using vehicles, road signs, trains, and homemade items, such as a cardboard rocket. Other good accessories are measuring tools (see Tools for Measurement, pages 80-81). Keep in mind that the purpose of a Block Center is to work with blocks, so limit the number of accessories you add at one time to four or five. It will keep the children's focus on building, and encourage them to use the accessories **after** construction.

One accessory that you should keep in the Block Center at all times is a container filled with paper, index cards, pencils, pens, markers, clear plastic tape, and pre-made, blank storybooks. Children can use these materials to make spontaneous signs and labels, write stories, or draw a picture.

Look at the letter for parents on page 46, which requests contributions for accessories. Look at the variety of objects listed. Variety changes the nature of the play. For example, children can transform cardboard cylinders into tunnels, fences, smoke stacks, and towers. They can turn boxes into rooms, trucks, barns, and building bases. They can make berry baskets into cages and greenhouses, tongue depressors into ladders, and film canisters into trashcans. Styrofoam peanuts can become snow or boulders!

Consider buying clear, plastic boxes with tops to store the accessories. Or, place the accessories in shoeboxes and mount a photograph or picture of the accessory on the side of the box. (Note: School-supply catalogs are a good source for photographs.) If the accessory is too large to fit into a shoebox, draw the object on an index card and tape it to the shelf where it belongs. Place the accessory containers on the top shelf so children can clearly see their choices.

Observe the children as they play. Think about how you can enhance what they are doing. At the same time, observe what they are not using and remove it. If the children aren't using what you have added, add something else. Children communicate through their behavior, allowing you to draw reliable inferences from what they do.

Accessories are the "gates" children go through to enter the realm of imaginative play. Every child needs imaginative "exercise." Some children have a lot of imagination, while others think more concretely. One never knows what accessory will strike a particular child's imagination. New accessories invite renewed interest. Experiment and see what works best.

The next chapter is about what to do after you set up the Block Center.

What Do I Do Now?

Chapter 3

(Or The Teacher's Job)

After setting up the Block Center, you might ask, "What do I do now?" This is a good question, and one that suggests your role will change. It does. You will take on a different role by becoming a facilitator of learning. This entails making the new surroundings of the Block Center meaningful and understandable to children. It also means making it safe for them as they work, either alone or in groups.

As a facilitator, your role will also include calming children when tempers erupt and helping them over hurdles that stand in their way of learning new things. In addition, you will also model the behavior you want imitated and negotiate and pose questions. Let's discuss these tasks.

Modeling

Children do what they see, and seeing adults do things piques their curiosity. If they observe you doing something, invariably they will want to do it too.

In past years, when I found that children were not choosing to play in the Block Center, I went to build in the Block Center myself. At first, the children would wander over and look. Then one or two would plop down beside me, look up and smile, and push a few blocks around on the floor. After a few minutes passed, two or three more would drop by. Soon, a group of children would be centered on the action, waiting for their turn.

I erected simple structures, such as one block on top of two, two side-by-side with a space in between, or a row of blocks. Nothing complicated. I have found that complicated structures intimidate children, inviting them to say to themselves, "I can't do that, so I won't build." Children seem to rule out things early in their school careers, usually due to some embarrassing moment when they felt that they did not measure up in some way. To prevent this from happening, begin with simple block building. Children are often encouraged by simplicity and by your positive actions.

Remember, too, that children love to follow a significant adult. Teachers are significant in the lives of the children in their classrooms. Don't underestimate your power to persuade through action. The children are watching, and seeing you build in the Block Center will draw them like a magnet. You may have to do it two or three times, depending on the group, but soon they will start building on their own.

One year my classroom block-builders hit a "building slump." They were stuck in the same old rut! To get them excited and doing things again, I moved some toys into the Block Center, including a house, garage, school, and an airport. One morning before the children arrived, I completed a simple "cityscape" using blocks. I made a road out of blocks that went through the city, with signs such as "Stop," "Yield," and "No U-turn." I placed small cars among the buildings and on the block road. When it was time for the children to go to the various centers, all of them wanted to go to the Block Center. We sorted it out, and groups of five took turns being "city builders." As they played, stacked, rebuilt, and moved things around, their enthusiasm blossomed. The next day, they built their own city, with roads and buildings spreading out in every direction. Gradually, the toys that I had put in the Block Center were pushed out. They wanted their own stuff! All they needed was a nudge and a few new ideas, and off they went!

Negotiating

No matter how well you organize and plan your Block Center, there will be conflicts between the children. Why? Because children get impatient waiting, they knock down buildings (accidentally and on purpose), and two children may want the same blocks. Disagreements may also erupt over designs for a group-building project. Because these disagreements are "real-life" issues to the children, they offer you unique opportunities to teach conflict-resolution skills. These are the first steps of negotiation and finding alternative solutions to the vexing problems of living with others. Remember, solutions must be win-win.

Children can learn that success is found in the art of compromise and by giving the other person the benefit of the doubt. For example, among the first things you can teach a young child is that a knocked-down building may not have been a deliberate act. A good assumption for them to make is that it was an accident. Accidents happen! Teaching children how to respond to accidents is a good first step toward resolving conflict early in an incident. They learn to assume a better "motive," rather than the worst. In turn, the child who "did it" may respond constructively to the child who has been "damaged." For example, he may say, "I'm sorry (I knocked your building down). Can I help you put it back up?" Model the behavior yourself.

When there is a legitimate dispute over blocks or turf, watch the progression, and then suggest alternatives to the children's solutions. Ask the children to come up with three possible solutions to the problem. Ask them to try each one and see which one works best.

Get a feel for **how** to get involved by *watching the action* **before** you attempt to influence it. Sometimes you won't understand what the problem is. Other times, you will have to help the children express their feelings. Many children don't have the words (or the permission to use them) to express how they feel or to ask for what they want. When you facilitate problem identification and offer possible solutions, you offer them their first skills in a lifetime of similar learning.

Challenging Children's Thinking

Encourage the children to take another step—to move beyond the level at which they are currently functioning— by asking them questions. There are many questions you can ask to encourage children to think at higher levels. The basic level of thinking is the *knowledge* level, so start by asking questions that require the child to recall small amounts of information. The next level, *comprehension,* requires the child to talk about the meaning of what happened. The third level of thinking is *application.* Ask, "How else could you use that?" Knowledge, comprehension, and application are basic levels of thinking. Taking the next step requires children to move into more advanced levels of thinking, ones that require more processing of the information held in their heads. This takes work.

You can evoke higher levels of thinking by asking questions requiring *analysis, synthesis,* and *evaluation.* Let's discuss each one separately.

Analysis requires breaking things down into their component parts to determine how they contribute to the whole thing. To invite analysis thinking in the Block Center, ask children:

- ✔ How do you know this is a _____?
- ✔ In which group does this _____ belong?
- ✔ How are these _____ the same? Different?
- ✔ Is this a _____ or a _____?

The next level of thinking is *synthesis,* or putting the parts of things together in a new way to form a new whole. In terms of blocks, children may use the same blocks to make something completely different. Useful questions to ask include:

- ✔ Can you think of a new way to _____?
- ✔ Can you tell me a story about _____?

✔ Can you draw a picture of a _____?

✔ How could you _____?

✔ Pretend you are a _____. Would you live in a _____ or would you live in a _____? What would you be like? Feel like? Look like? How would you talk?

In the Block Center, there are no right answers. Activities are open-ended and children are free to change direction. They can pretend, invent, and improvise. The purpose of the teacher's questions is to encourage children's thinking. By asking certain questions, you can help children achieve *evaluation,* the highest level of thinking. Evaluation is a child's ability to judge the value of material for a given purpose. Their judgments are based on specific criteria. Examples of questions are:

✔ Are blocks good for making clothes? Why not? What makes clothes good? Are clothes soft? Are blocks soft?

✔ Could you stick your arm into an armhole in a block? What things have armholes? Do blocks have pockets? If something has pockets, what would it be?

You can phrase other questions to elicit evaluation responses, such as:

✔ Which _____ do you like the best? Why?

✔ What do (don't) you like about _____? Why?

✔ What is the best (worst) thing about _____? Why?

While you do not want to overwhelm a child by asking questions, you do want to look for teachable moments to ask a question or two. The questions can invite the child to move to a more advanced level of thinking.

The next chapter is about assessing children's learning in the Block Center.

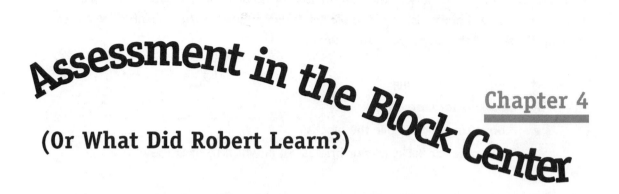

Assessment in the Block Center
(Or What Did Robert Learn?)

Chapter 4

In the Introduction of this book, I said that Robert learned most of what he needed to know by playing in the Block Center. How do I know that? I found out through assessment. First, I learned what he already knew. When he was ready, I added things to challenge him.

At first, I did not know what to look for when Robert was building with the blocks. In time, I realized that there are stages of block play. The following information about the stages of block play is essential for assessing what children are learning. Learning the stages helped me understand Robert's developmental progress. (Ages are approximate.)

The Stages of Block Play

THE STAGES OF BLOCK PLAY

Stage One: Discovering Blocks

Stage Two: Stacking Blocks

Stage Three: Creating Bridges

Stage Four: Making Enclosures

Stage Five: Using Patterns and Symmetry

Stage Six: Designing, Planning, and Constructing
      Elaborate Structures

Stage One (Ages 2-3): In this stage, children carry, move, touch, hold, pile, knock down, drop, and feel the blocks. Children do little or no building. Instead, they explore the properties and characteristics of the blocks. Children answer the question, "What can I do with these?" At this stage, you can provide:

- ✔ wagons for hauling
- ✔ baskets for carrying
- ✔ boxes in which to pile the blocks
- ✔ suitcases (or backpacks or briefcases) in which to pack the blocks

Stage Two (Age 3): In this stage, children stack blocks vertically, lay them down and line them up, or configure them horizontally. One block may be laid across another. Children will often repeat a pattern over and over. "Stack and Row" is a good name for this stage. Many times, you will observe children forming a combination of stacks and rows. At this stage, you can provide:

- ✔ pattern cards, so the child can copy it with blocks
- ✔ cars and road signs
- ✔ floor mats on which to build
- ✔ a large piece of poster board, with a large triangle in the center, so she can build within the triangle

Stage Three (Ages 3-4): This stage is known as bridging. It is the stage when children begin to make structures. Bridging is when children form a space between two blocks, and then place a block to span the space. Eventually, as the child masters and expands bridging, her bridges become more elaborate. Typically, the child will build in the stacks and rows she previously made and add the bridges. At this stage, you can provide:

- ✔ pictures of bridges
- ✔ architectural drawings that show bridging concepts
- ✔ a large piece of blue cloth (symbolizing water) and boats
- ✔ columns (typically used for elaborate cake decorating)

Stage Four (Age 4): This stage involves making enclosures. At this stage, children can close up a space between blocks with another block(s). Children begin problem solving by planning ahead how they will close up spaces. After mastering enclosures by lying the blocks flat on the floor, children make an enclosure by standing the blocks on edge, and they may incorporate bridging. They discover and begin to understand the meaning of *inside*, *outside*, *perimeter*, and *boundaries*. They also observe balance and symmetry. Children add figures, which take on imaginary roles as children play out social motifs that are meaningful to them. At this stage, you can provide:

- ✔ farm and zoo animals
- ✔ fruits and vegetables to make a fruit and vegetable stand
- ✔ a length of fabric or ribbon (to drape vertical enclosures)
- ✔ posters and photographs of buildings (especially those that show enclosures as elements of a structure)

Stage Five (Ages 4-5): This is the stage where children begin making elaborate, decorative structures. For example, the child may incorporate a bathtub, store, farmyard, and swing into the same structure. Often, children name their structures (although the names rarely define the building's function). Patterns emerge in children's structures, and symmetry is more intricate. The child starts to classify, sort, and match shapes and sizes. At this stage, you can provide:

- ✔ large task cards, made from magazine photographs of different buildings
- ✔ "skyscrapers" (tall buildings) made from cardboard boxes
- ✔ blank paper to make signs and labels
- ✔ roofing materials
- ✔ photographs of famous paintings or structures
- ✔ color cubes
- ✔ blank storybooks to write about the constructions

Stage Six (Ages 5-6 and older): At this stage, children work cooperatively to build a structure, deciding in advance what they will build. They build their structures to look much like what they have planned in advance. Due to the complexity of the structure and the commitment of the children, they typically want to build and play with the structure over a period of several days. The children assign each other roles, and they use a variety of materials to achieve desired effects. At this stage, children excel at sorting, matching, classifying, and arranging patterns. They will also begin dramatic play around the block structure. At this stage, you can provide:

- ✔ a variety of hats and clothes
- ✔ measuring tools
- ✔ small task cards
- ✔ block building books
- ✔ home building magazines
- ✔ blueprints
- ✔ candles without wicks
- ✔ beanbag figures

Assessing Robert in the Block Center

Knowing the developmental stages of block play helped me know what Robert was capable of doing. It also provided clues about how I could help him move from one stage to the next. I learned, for example, that I could not say to Robert, "Why don't you make a sign for your building?" (a Stage Five task) when he was in Stage Two. What I could do, though, was help him focus on the patterns he was making with the blocks. I could also add cars, street signs, and a measuring mat in the Block Center. These accessories would help Robert build successfully at his developmental stage while keeping him interested. I could track Robert's development throughout the year by observing what he was doing in the Block Center. At each stage, I could add new accessories to help him build new skills.

Let's review Robert's progression of block building throughout the school year. He began his block building at Stage One. He carried around the blocks and shuffled them around on the floor in a deliberate way. He seemed to ask himself, "Now, what can I do with these?" He explored the wood texture, weight, fit, and shapes of the blocks.

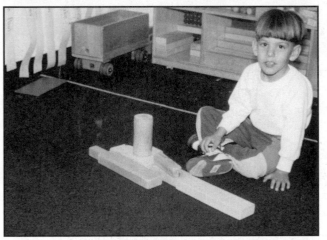

As the year progressed, he began to stack the blocks and purposefully lay them out on the floor.

By December, Robert was bridging. To do this, Robert had to estimate the length of the blocks and the space to bridge before beginning construction. After estimating the space and setting the blocks, he made successful bridges. He began to fine-tune his estimates and became more accurate.

By February, Robert was making enclosures (demonstrating spatial awareness) and arriving at unique solutions to form a closed, box-like structure.

By April, Robert developed his enclosures into more complex structures. Robert used stack and row construction, bridging, and enclosures to construct an elaborate building, which he called "The Store." It had a barn on one end and a bathroom on the other.

By May, Robert and his friend were working collaboratively to make "A Farm." They decided on the idea after much discussion and negotiation. They designed and built it as agreed! During the building, both children made many compromises, and both were satisfied with how the finished construction looked. They were pleased with their collaboration; so was I. What a celebration of growth for Robert!

I used the Stages of Block Play to track Robert's development. At each point, I knew what to expect next from him. I also was able to document his growth and change over time as he played in the place in which he was most comfortable.

In the first chapter of this book, I listed all the skills children learn in the Block Center. To help Robert develop these skills, I added accessories and collateral activities when

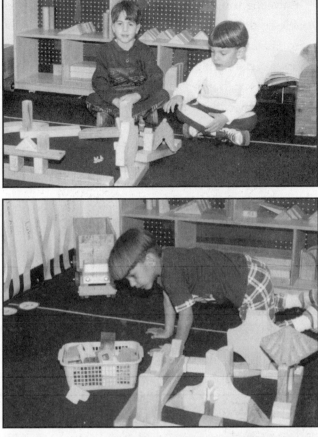

he was ready for them, which I knew from the Stages of Block Play. However, to find out what Robert learned, I had to learn how to assess children's play in the Block Center. Portfolio assessment provided the documentation that Robert was learning what he needed to learn.

How to Do Assessment in the Block Center

I used portfolios as my classroom assessment tool. In the children's portfolios, I included photographs, information from the parents, tape recordings, checklists, anecdotal records, and work samples. I used many methods of gathering information about each child so I could get a portrait of each one.

Photographs: Block constructions cannot be saved for more than a few days, so taking photographs is a good way to capture the skills a child learns over time. Photographs helped me to capture Robert's developmental stages of play and the various skills he learned. However, taking photographs is expensive, so you cannot use them exclusively.

Information from Parents: Ask parents to contribute drawings or stories their children create at home about building with blocks. If parents take photographs of their children's constructions, also add these to their portfolio.

Tape Recordings: Before Robert had the skills to write a story, I made tape recordings of his original stories. For example, he would dictate a story about how he built his structure, giving me as many details as possible. Later, as he worked, he made up stories that he dictated into the tape recorder. His recordings provided me with information about his language development, his sentence structure, and his vocabulary.

Checklists: I made a brief checklist from the progress-reporting instrument (checklist, narrative, or report card) that goes home to parents (see page 12). Choose a few skills to measure regularly in the Block Center. One drawback of using checklists is that they allow for only "Yes" or "No" responses—that is, either the child can or cannot do it. I modified the checklist to include more information, including a box that indicates that extra documentation could be found in the portfolio.

Anecdotal Records: These records are brief, factual statements written in narrative form. I could make notes, for example, that Robert had: (1) created an A, B, A, B pattern; (2) matched the blocks to their silhouettes; (3) counted blocks;

and (4) placed one triangular block on one unit block (which showed an understanding of one-to-one correspondence). I made an anecdotal record of what Robert did, which showed what he did know and what he still needed to learn. For example, "Robert placed the blocks in a line, and counted 1, 2, 5, 8, 22." This told me that Robert was learning to count and could put things in number sequence, but needed additional help learning the exact sequence of numbers.

ROBERT   BLOCK CENTER   3/14/00   9:45

Robert took the measuring tape from the shelf and asked Javier to hold one end. (He wanted to measure how far it was from his house of blocks to Javier's.) He measured and said, "We are three feets from each other."

My interpretation of the anecdotal record: Robert understood that the tape was a measuring tool. He read numbers in feet, and he recognized the number "3" on the measuring tape.

My plan: Work on the difference between the singular "foot" and the plural "feet." Encourage him to measure other blocks and other objects that were around him.

Work Samples: I looked for opportunities to gather Robert's work samples. Some examples are when Robert made a sign for his building (see sample #1), showing letter awareness. He was starting to write by using the sounds of letters. When he drew a picture of his structure or when he wrote a story about it, I saved it or made a copy for his portfolio. I always asked his permission to include work in his portfolio—an excellent way to keep him involved in his own learning.

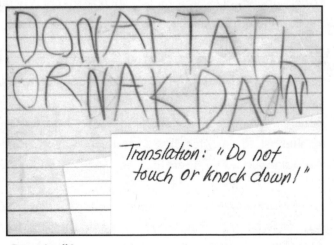

Translation: "Do not touch or knock down!"

Sample #1

Robert's work samples provided me with information about his ability to form words and about his understanding that words represent thoughts. I also was able to determine if

The ambulance went to look for the man but he wasn't in there.

"Movie picture show where you see 'Lion king'"

5/12

Robert understood "storyness," such as, did his characters move through his story? Did the story make sense? Did the story have a beginning, middle, and an end?

As I mentioned earlier, by May, Robert was able to draw a plan for a future block construction, and then execute the plan. I kept a copy of his plan and added it to his portfolio.

Robert moved on to kindergarten and his portfolio went with him. His kindergarten teacher asked me why all of the information about Robert came from the Block Center. We discussed how Robert learned best. She understood.

Robert is now a successful student in the second grade. In the beginning, blocks offered a way for Robert to adjust to school. Later, they provided a way for him to learn necessary skills. Through observation and documentation, I was able to let Robert learn in the style that best suited him.

Tips for Assessing Children in the Block Center

1. Take photographs to document that the child is learning a skill and is grasping a concept. For example, if a child places a triangular block on top of a unit block several times, take a photo and make a note that she understands one-to-one correspondence. Hang a "Photograph Log" on a wall, and write the number of the photograph and a brief description. For example:

   "Photograph 3 showed (child's name) doing _____. Photograph 14 showed him _____."

   It may take at least several weeks before you get the photographs developed, so the notes will remind you where you are in the assessment process of each child.

2. Collect work samples. Make available paper, pencils, and clear plastic tape for children to make signs and labels; blank paper books for them to write about their constructions; and large sheets of paper for them to draw pictures. Photocopy or save the work and include it in their portfolios. The work samples you collect over time will capture the child's progress in writing development, their concept of "storyness," and their ability to understand that photographs and drawings are representations of objects.

3. Make anecdotal records. Write factual, non-judgmental observations of a child's activity in narrative form. Write the child's name, date, time, and location of the activity. Describe what you see in detail. When you observe an emerging skill (or one that a child is repeating), make a note of it.

4. Make audio recordings of events. Keep a tape recorder and tapes for each child in the Block Center. Ask the child to tell a story about her structure or make up a song about what's going on in her building. Or she could describe how she made her building or how it functions. These tape recordings will help you assess a child's oral language development, sentence structure, speech, and vocabulary.

5. Develop your own checklist. Extract some of the skills and concepts from your progress-reporting instrument and form a list of items that can be answered "Yes" or "No." When a child masters a skill, check it off. Include skills and concepts that require little or no back-up documentation.

6. Include information from parents. Add notes sent in from parents, as well as drawings or photographs brought from home. These will add variety to the child's skills portrait. Parents will enjoy sharing the assessment process if they understand its value and purpose.

Now that you know how to assess a child, turn to the next chapter and learn how to involve the child's first and most important teachers—the parents.

Involving Parents

(Or Taking Blocks Home)

Chapter 5

Parents are children's first and most important teachers. Robert's parents understood that the Block Center was a good way to channel information to him. They contributed to our "junk" list of accessories and, occasionally, they came to build in the Block Center with Robert.

To fully complete the loop in the education process, teachers need to let parents know not only *what* is going on in the classroom, but *why*. The "why" gives parents a reason to build on what you are doing in the classroom. For example, if the children are using blocks at school, ask parents if they can have them at home, too. If they cannot buy blocks, they can make them. Send home block activities for parents to do with their child. Parents will feel more successful when they know what is going on, how they can contribute, and why it is worth the effort. Good ideas work at home or school!

Another benefit of involving parents is that when they understand what is happening in the classroom and why, they are more likely to cooperate with the school and the teachers. Parental understanding is worth a lot. Look at the following example. Suppose a mother asks her child, "What did you do today?" Her child responds, "Played with blocks." The mother thinks to herself, "I sent my child to school to learn to read, write, and do math. What's this block stuff?" The next day, the mother calls the teacher for an explanation. This is where your preparatory work will pay off—by preventing possible misunderstandings *before* they occur. If you spend some time educating parents on the value of block play, you will be rewarded substantially over the year.

Let parents know what children learn when they play and build in the Block Center. Look at the Introductory Parent Letter on page 44. Copy or modify it as desired, but send a letter home at the *beginning* of the school year to let parents know what is going on at school.

Dear Parents,

Come and see our Block Center! Your child will be coming home and sharing stories about building in the Block Center. However, building with blocks is not the only thing your child will be doing there. He or she also will be learning reading, writing, math, language development, and social skills. How? Let me explain.

▸ By planning and organizing his or her construction before building with blocks, your child will be learning pre-reading and writing skills. For example, he or she may be asked to write stories about how to build his or her structures.

▸ When your child builds a structure to represent a real-life object, such as a garage, he or she is learning that several things put together can represent one thing. For example, your child will use several blocks to make one garage. This concept is similar to putting letters together to make a word, which is a basic skill of reading.

▸ As your child builds with blocks, he or she works with patterns, sequences, and symmetry. This will help him or her to develop important math skills.

▸ Math occurs naturally when your child works with blocks. This is because the blocks are in mathematical proportion. Therefore, when your child works with blocks, he or she develops an understanding of fractions, part-and-whole relationships, shapes, and counting.

▸ When your child works with other children to build structures, they work collaboratively by sharing their ideas and plans. This helps your child to learn the value of sharing, taking turns, and working cooperatively.

The Block Center is one of the most popular places in the classroom. Fortunately, it is also one of the best places for your child to learn the skills that will make him or her a successful learner.

Come take a look! If you want, you can build, too!

Sincerely,

As I suggested before, encourage parents to keep blocks at home. When they observe their children playing with blocks, they will be able to see for themselves how much learning occurs.

Another way to foster parents' interest and understanding, and encourage cooperation, is to ask for recycled contributions. Most parents want to contribute to school projects. Asking them to donate recycled items is great for two reasons: it lets them contribute to block building, and it encourages conservation. It won't cost them any money, and it takes very little time. And lastly, encourage them to come in and build with their child one day.

Get parents involved and ask for their help. If a parent works with wood, he or she might be willing to make wood blocks for the classroom. Other parents might be willing to sand some of the rough edges of the blocks at home. Some might be able to help make accessories for the Block Center.

Send parents the letter on page 46. When parents respond to the letter, they become involved by saving things and sending them to school.

Dear Parents,

We need "junk" for the Block Center!

Below is a list of things you can send to school. When? Anytime! Please post it near your trashcan, so you can refer to it when you're throwing away something we could use. Don't automatically throw it out—it could be valuable junk!

berry baskets
bricks
cardboard cylinders
carpet squares
coffee can lids
cotton
dollhouse accessories
egg cartons
empty thread spools
fake Easter grass
fast food boxes
felt scraps
film canisters
furniture protectors
linoleum scraps
margarine tubs
oatmeal boxes
old blanket
old cars
pieces of cellophane
pieces of fabric
pipe cleaners
plastic animals
Popsicle sticks
shoeboxes
Styrofoam meat trays
Styrofoam peanuts

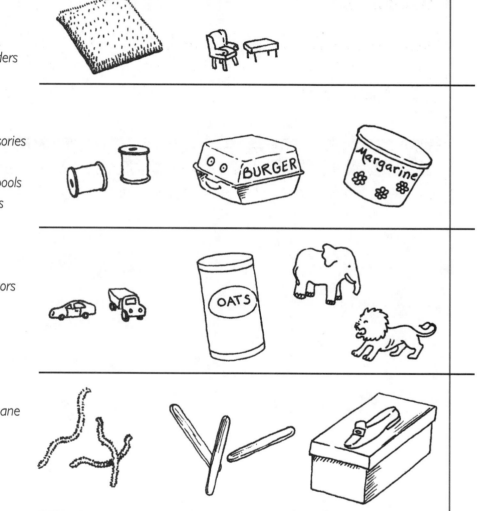

If you can think of anything else we could use, toss it in a bag, and have your child bring it to school. Your contributions will enrich our Block Center. Stop by and see us anytime!

Sincerely,

After you have emphasized to parents what block play teaches their children, and after you have encouraged them to be interested in blocks, send home the letter below and the instructions for making blocks on pages 48-51. The parent(s) may consider making or buying blocks for their child to use at home.

Dear Parents,

Blocks offer your child many ways to learn different skills, such as reading, writing, math, and problem solving. For example, your child learns math by measuring the things he or she builds. Your child might describe the size of his or her building as "four blocks long and two blocks wide."

If you do not have blocks at home, don't let that stop your child's block play. Enclosed are ideas that you can use to make blocks at home. Give the ideas a try. You might even find yourself on the floor with your child—building your own garage, with a house attached!

Sincerely,

Milk Carton Blocks

1. Collect two of each of these sizes of milk cartons: ½ pint (240 ml), 1 pint (0.5 L), 1 quart (1 L), and ½ gallon (2 L). Rinse them thoroughly in soapy water.

2. Cut off the tops of the cartons to make them into elongated rectangles.

3. Fill one of each pair of cartons with Styrofoam packing peanuts or newspaper strips. Fit the matching empty carton over the filled carton. Remove about 2" (5 cm) of the corners. This will allow you to slide the filled carton into the empty carton easily.

4. Securely tape the boxes together. Cover the boxes with contact paper to make them last indefinitely.

① quart ½ pint pint ½ gallon

② cut off the top....

③

④ full box · empty box

slide empty box over full box, enclosing "stuffing" inside.

⑤ seal with tape.

cover box with paper.

Detergent Box Blocks

1. Collect a variety of boxes—ranging from large detergent boxes to small gift boxes.

2. Fill each box with Styrofoam packing peanuts or newspaper strips.

3. Tape each box well and cover it with contact paper.

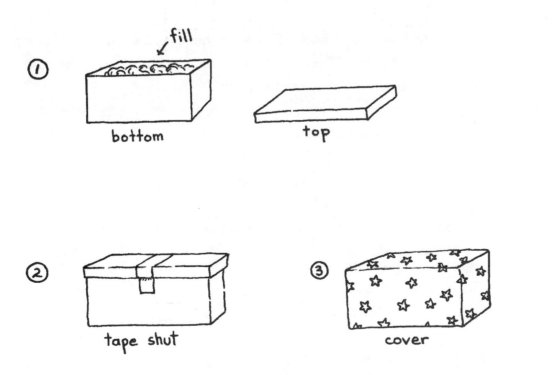

① fill

bottom   top

② tape shut

③ cover

Paper Bag Blocks

1. Collect large, brown paper grocery sacks.

2. Fill the sacks with newspaper strips and tightly pack them in.

3. Fold over the top of the sacks and securely tape them closed.

Styrofoam Blocks Wrapped in Cloth

1. Measure, mark, and cut Styrofoam into 4" (10 cm) cubes. (Use a serrated bread knife to cut the Styrofoam.)

2. Cut a piece of cloth into one 17" x 5" (42 cm x 12 cm) strip and two 5" x 5" (12 cm x 12 cm) square strips.

3. Create the sides of the cube. Sew the short ends of the 17" x 5" (42 cm x 12 cm) strip together, overlapping the ends ½" (1 cm).

4. Create the bottom of the cube. Sew one of the two 5" x 5" (12 cm x 12 cm) squares to the 17" x 5" (42 cm x 12 cm) cloth strip as shown in the illustration, overlapping it at the seams ½" (1 cm).

5. Turn the cloth right side out.

6. Sew one side of the top flap to the cloth.

7. Insert the Styrofoam square and sew together all of the remaining seams to make a six-sided cube.

①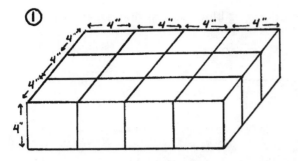

cut a 16×12×4" block of styrofoam into 12 blocks, measuring 4×4×4".

②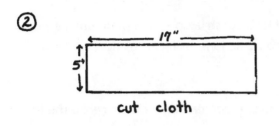

17"

5"

cut cloth

③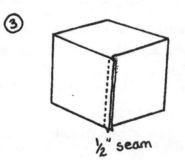

½" seam

④

bottom

½" seam

⑥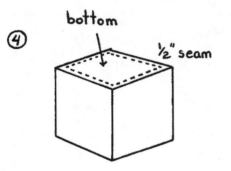

sew top flap

styrofoam block

⑦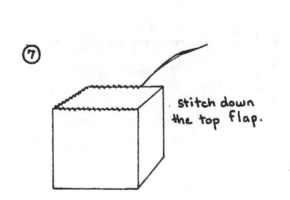

stitch down the top flap.

Once parents have shown an interest in encouraging block play at home, send them the following letter.

Dear Parents,
Your child is becoming a master block-builder.

He or she has made tall, short, wide, and long constructions. He or she made simple structures, as well as more complicated constructions, using items donated to the Block Center.

At school, when your child builds with others, together they read or recite the following poem. Maybe you and child would enjoy reading the poem together, too.

Blocks by Sharon MacDonald

I'm building a house
Wide and tall.
I'm making a yard
With a garden and wall.

I'm stacking the blocks
Big and small.
To make all the rooms
And a very long hall.

I'm putting the blocks
In a square all 'round,
In just the right places
So they won't fall down.

I have to build fast,
So there's time to play.
I'm all packed and ready
To move in today!

Activities to Do at Home

1. Read the poem and discuss what it would be like to live in a block house. What would the rooms look like? What about the garden wall? The hall? The doorways?

2. Draw a picture of the block house described in the poem. Draw part of the house, and then ask your child to draw the other part.

3. Give your child a magazine and blunt-tipped scissors. Encourage him or her to cut out pictures of different buildings. Talk about the similarities and differences between each building and the house in the poem.

4. Save boxes of various sizes and let your child build with them.

5. Check out a library book about building things.

Sincerely,

The time that you spend encouraging parents to work with their children at home is time well spent. The knowledge that you influenced some parents to work with their children is no small accomplishment considering all of the other distractions at home. And blocks can be fun for parents, too. Parents probably have plenty of ideas left over from their own childhood to try out and share.

Turn to the next chapter to read about using other construction materials.

Using Other Construction Materials

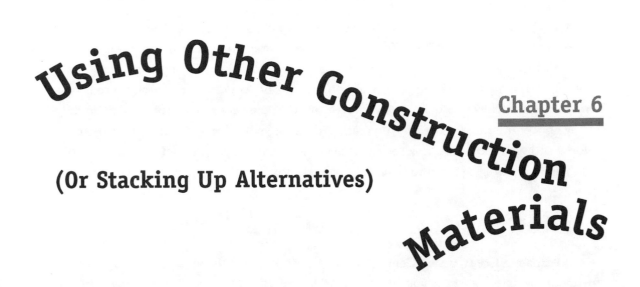

Chapter 6

(Or Stacking Up Alternatives)

I often wonder what I would have done if I had not had a Block Center for Robert. I would have encouraged him in other ways, using alternatives to unit blocks. Other construction products and materials are available; they make excellent alternatives to unit blocks. Alternatives fall into two categories: some develop fine motor skills, while others develop gross motor skills.

Unit Blocks Are Best

Please keep in mind that I have a bias toward using unit blocks over other construction materials in the early childhood years. For one thing, unit blocks are in direct mathematical proportion, whereas construction materials are not. This helps children learn many math skills. Children also use different muscles when they build with unit blocks as opposed to construction materials. Because unit blocks are comparatively heavy, children use large muscles, such as the back, shoulders, upper and lower legs, and arms. They must develop strength and control to successfully manipulate the blocks. Young children are more able to use their big muscles than their smaller ones. Construction materials, on the other hand, require children to use fine motor control, which is typically lagging in the young child. This is why many young children are not ready to tie their shoes. Using small finger muscles, such as moving the thumb against the fingertips, involves a specific brain function, which is usually not adequately developed in younger children. Therefore, they may not be as successful with these materials as they are manipulating unit blocks.

Advantages of Other Construction Materials

Working with other construction materials helps children develop fine motor skills and learn to solve unique problems. These solutions are often complicated. Children must think of new ways to get things to go together—they learn to be young engineers. The use of these materials also nurtures children's creativity. As with unit blocks, there is no right way for children to build, so they focus on what they are doing, not how to do it. They concentrate and come up with unique ideas. By exploring and discovering what works and what does not, children must think simultaneously about different aspects of a problem, encouraging them to think "outside the box."

Creating a Construction Center

To create a Construction Center, I used the list of materials on pages 57-58. I used many of the same behavior guidelines as I did for the Block Center. For example, children may knock down only what they have built. I also defined the workspace with a small rug to keep children working in one place. The child puts the bucket or tub of materials on the rug and works. However, there are some differences in the Construction Center.

First of all, the Construction Center takes up much less classroom space than the Block Center. If necessary, you can set it up on one table. I put the materials in dishpans or small tubs so the children can dig around and look for what they want, without having to dump out all of the pieces. I use the same dishpans over and over so the children will know from a glance what they contain. I only put out one material at a time, because there are so many pieces involved. When the materials are not in use, I store them in large, resealable plastic bags. To challenge the children, I change the materials every two to three weeks. During the first few days of putting out a new material, I watch to see how much it is being used. If the children aren't using the Center, I change what is in it, even if the materials have been out for only a day or two.

In addition to the construction materials mentioned on pages 57-58, you can also use homemade materials. These include pieces of cardboard, Styrofoam pieces, PVC pipe segments (elbows and connectors), furniture-packing corners, pillows, sponges, paper cups, thread spools, and boxes—the larger the better! (The activities on pages 144-163 show you how to use these materials.)

Other than paper and pencil for making signs, I add few accessories to the Construction Center.

When deciding which materials to put in the Construction Center, match the level of difficulty of the materials to the ability of the children. For example, think about the fine motor skills the children have and decide if they have the skills to do a particular activity.

You want to challenge them, but not frustrate them to the point of giving up before they have experienced some success. Some children give up more quickly than others, so observe what each child is trying to do. If a child has advanced fine motor skills, for example, give her more advanced construction materials, such as Legos. Provide a child with less developed fine motor skills with products that are large and easy to grasp.

The following age guidelines are approximate. Many children are capable of doing more difficult work at the ages specified. Be prepared to challenge children with more advanced work and to change materials so children will be successful.

Suggested Materials for Different Age Groups

✔ For two- and three-year-olds: Pillows, large Legos, cardboard boxes, paper bags, boxes, and other easy-to-grasp large materials. These materials do not require highly developed fine motor skills.

✔ For three- and young four-year-olds: Stacking materials (smaller than the ones above), spools, furniture corners, paper cups, 1" (2 cm) cubes, and small boxes.

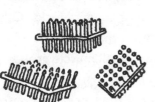

✔ For two-, three-, and young four-year-olds: Bristle Blocks, Triangles, Krinkles, or similar materials (those that stick together by pushing them together). These materials offer children opportunities to grasp and press, and then pull the pieces apart. Children use more hand and less finger work. These are not as precise as Tinkertoys, Pegs, and Wheels and Rings (following).

✔ For some three-, four- and five-year-olds: Tinkertoys, Pegs, and Wheels and Rings. Each of these activities requires the child to push a stick into a small hole. This movement requires precise execution and eye-hand coordination.

✔ For older four- and five-year-olds: Small Legos, Ringamajigs, Form-A-Tions, Ji-Gan-Tiks, and any of the interlocking, snap-together blocks. These materials are great for developing small hand muscles. The required pulling, pushing, and connecting help the child use her brain and fingers to manipulate small things and to concentrate. Good eye-hand coordination also is required because the work is precise.

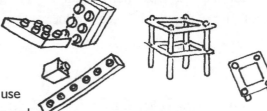

✔ For older four-, five-, and six-year-olds: Lincoln Logs, Gears, and similar products with interlocking pieces that require balancing and complex problem solving. These materials are ideal for this age group because they require finger control, eye-hand coordination, and the ability to "see-what-you-want-in-your-head-before-you-make-it."

✔ For five-, six-, and seven-year-olds: Erector Sets, PVC pipes with connectors, and any of the materials that require extensive, controlled use of the hand and fingers. These products require balancing while grasping, twisting, and pinching at the same time. The child must be able to focus for long periods of time and to coordinate the use of both hands at the same time.

Construction Materials That Develop Fine Motor Skills

Some of the products that exercise fine motor skills are Legos, Tinkertoys, Bristle Blocks, Krinkles, Unifix Cubes, Ji-Gan-Tinks, Lock Blocks, Gears, Lincoln Logs, One-Inch Cubes, and Erector Sets. Some of these products offer building characteristics that are similar to unit blocks. Others, however, are small with components that children assemble rather than construct. Assembly requires children to have well-developed fine motor skills (the small muscle groups of the fingers and hands).

All of the block and construction materials mentioned offer valuable teaching opportunities. Think of them as learning tools.

When selecting which products to use, remember that they should encourage free play and that activities need to be open-ended—there is no "right way" to do an activity and no particular conclusion. It is up to the child to decide when she is through. Activities should take the child wherever her imagination and creativity take her. Alternative construction materials offer children many chances to learn many of the concepts discussed in this book. For example, children develop fine motor skills (the skills that use the thumb and forefinger in a pincher-like way) by fastening, twisting, turning, pushing, and fitting small pieces together. These products also can be used in ways similar to unit blocks.

Construction Materials That Develop Gross Motor Skills

When unit blocks are not available, both brick-pattern cardboard blocks or hollow wooden blocks are good alternatives. These larger construction materials require children to use larger muscle groups, including the shoulders, arms, back, buttocks, and legs. Children under the age of five usually have sufficient gross motor skill development (larger muscle groups) to manage the blocks nicely.

Brick-pattern blocks are inexpensive and surprisingly lightweight and durable. They come in three and sometimes four different colors. Because they fall over more easily than unit blocks, it is best to use these blocks on a hard surface. Fortunately, they don't make a lot of noise when a child knocks over a stack. (This is important, especially when the children are not building on a carpeted surface.) Children can use them to build structures for dramatic play or dramatize a story. For example, children can make boats to go sailing, fire trucks in which they can fight fires, and houses in which they can live. They can construct community places that invite useful and productive role-playing, such as pet stores where they can "buy" their favorite animal. When using brick-pattern cardboard blocks for dramatic play, provide the children with role-playing props as well. (See Props to Use with Block Play, pages 151-152 for suggestions.)

Playing with brick-pattern blocks helps children to develop their large muscles. As they build, they crawl, tiptoe, stretch, reach, and step over blocks and other children. In addition, they must use two hands to move the blocks, which forces them to use the two sides of their bodies together in a coordinated way. This is an important developmental achievement. As children develop this skill, they master the ability of using their whole body to accomplish a task. For example, when a child holds together a structure with her hands, arms, and chest and then reaches out her foot to slide an essential new component into place, she is using her whole body. Children develop balance, coordination, and symmetry through large block play. Another way brick-pattern blocks can help children learn to read is through pattern recognition—a building block of reading. Because the blocks are different colors, they invite pattern recognition because children learn to look for patterns.

As with unit blocks, the children move through the developmental stages of block play when they use brick-pattern cardboard blocks. The children can haul, stack-and-row, bridge, enclose, make structures, and work collaboratively to make things. Also, a child's developmental progress is revealed in the structures they build. Look for complexity and change as the children work.

CARING FOR BRICK-PATTERN CARDBOARD BLOCKS

Here are a few suggestions about caring for brick-pattern cardboard blocks:

* If two- to three-year-olds are going to be using the blocks, fill them with shredded newspaper, tape them closed, and cover them with clear, contact paper. Very

young children often sit on the blocks. Covering them with clear contact paper extends their life, allowing them to survive a few sit-downs by a young child. Filling them with newspaper makes it less likely that the blocks will fall over when the children build with them. This will reduce opportunities for frustration and hurt feelings. Use the blocks **indoors** only. The moisture outdoors will soften the cardboard, making the blocks fall apart.

* With four-, five-, and six-year-olds, discuss the care and use of the blocks. Explain to them that the blocks are for building, not sitting. Ask them to take down their structures one or two blocks at a time, and not to knock down a structure (even their own). Let them help you establish guidelines to follow when using the blocks. In addition, it might still be a good idea to fill them with newspaper or Styrofoam peanuts.

Another benefit of using brick-pattern blocks is that clean-up time can be a breeze, especially if you have taught the children to help. To make it more fun, you can put on a little music and sing a "work" song while putting away the blocks. The blocks are easy to store—just stack them in a corner, out of the way until the next use.

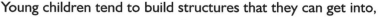

Another great alternative to unit blocks are hollow wooden blocks. They are similar to brick-pattern blocks, but they are made of wood. This makes them more durable, but also comparatively expensive and heavier than you might expect. They are also noisier to work with indoors, so they are best used over a carpeted area. As with brick-pattern block play, playing with hollow wooden blocks invites dramatic play. (See pages 151-152, Props to Use with Block Play, for props that work well with any kind of block—cardboard or wooden.)

Young children tend to build structures that they can get into, rather than structures to play with, so wooden blocks work well for this. Children often use them as chairs inside their constructions. While it is safe for them to do this, the hollow wooden blocks endure lots of wear and tear. Encourage children to bring chairs into their structures to sit on, rather than on the blocks themselves. Hollow wooden blocks come in many shapes, such as full and half squares, ramps, doubles, and short and long boards. There are also large-scale, see-through window blocks that are perfect for making bridges, tunnels, skyscrapers, and simple machines. (See Ramps and the Inclined Plane on pages 157-158 for a simple machine activity that works well with young children.)

It is best not to structure block activities. Instead, encourage the children to haul, tote, and build as they like. Because these blocks are heavy and cumbersome, simply manipulating them is a challenge for children and helps them to develop body awareness and movement skills. They learn coordination, using their arms and legs in tandem to accomplish a task. As they push and pull the blocks, they learn to use large muscle groups with precision as they bend, lift, tote, squat, reach, and stretch. Since the blocks are heavy, they are best used by four-, five-, and six-year-olds. Make sure they follow the same safety guidelines as with the unit blocks. The children need to understand that if blocks fall on them (or others), it can hurt. Emphasize that they are to build no taller than their own shoulders. Since children usually build while standing, this will substantially reduce the opportunity for a block to fall on a child's head.

To help make storing the blocks easier and more orderly, help the children make a storage-and-stacking pattern on paper and put it near where the blocks are stacked. The design on paper is actually an "expectations contract" with the children—they are expected to clean up and stack the blocks in a certain way in the assigned area. Making a stacking pattern is a lot of work for children since some of the blocks have unusual shapes. Encourage the children to explore different ways of stacking until they come up with the most efficient way of doing it. Involving the children gives structure and purpose to clean-up time and includes them in the ownership of cleaning up—an essential part of block play.

CARING FOR HOLLOW WOODEN BLOCKS
Rub the blocks with mineral oil and a soft cloth about once a year. If you use the blocks outside during the day, bring them indoors at night.

While many of the activities in this book are presented with unit blocks in mind, most can be easily used with other construction products and materials.

Remember, building with blocks or other construction materials develops skills for lifelong learning.

Making Connections to New Learning

(Or Block Tracks)

Chapter 7

This chapter is about how children can make connections to new learning—to extend what they know. While self-directed learning plays a large part in the education of young children, inserting structure into block play can help to extend children's learning. To accomplish this, the teacher must show the way.

Children need teachers to be their guides. As discussed in Chapter 3, the teacher acts as a facilitator and a model. For children to make connections and extensions of their knowledge base, more structured approaches are needed. Before we move on, however, let's review what we have covered so far.

We have discussed what children learn from block play, why it is important, how to make a place in your classroom or center for blocks, and how to encourage block play. In addition, you have learned ways to get parents more involved, how to assess the learning taking place, and how you can use other construction materials and products to teach children many of the skills learned with unit blocks.

Props and Accessories

Where do you go from there? You can add things, called props or accessories, that invite children to work with blocks in new ways. Because children are already interested in the blocks, the additions enhance the interest and eagerness that they already have for blocks. Most young children need to be interested and eager to focus on a subject; more complex experiences build on well-known ones. Blocks become a vehicle to new learning. For example, block play enables children to learn to **read,** do **science and math, get along with others,** and **work together collaboratively** in a group. They start learning these things by simply experimenting with the blocks. Then, with a teacher's guidance and direction, they can expand on these areas of the curriculum, acquiring new skills and learning new concepts. As you already know, play is learning. Some people "play" all their lives because the things they enjoy are embedded in their work. Blocks are like that.

Children know what to do with blocks—they need little help, instruction, or supervision. There comes a time, however, when the teacher must take on a structured role if children are to build **new** knowledge. An example is learning how to read. Teachers teach children how to read. When children learn the basic skills to unlock words, the teacher presents more complex words. Teachers provide the children with a toolbox of skills from which they grab solutions to new word problems. After children become fluent readers, they can learn by reading. Blocks are a lot like reading. Children learn the block basics (the skills necessary to unlock new problems) and are then presented with more complicated problems. The teacher must stage what happens and set the agenda. The challenge is knowing what accessories to add and when to add them.

When are children ready to take on new things? This is not an easy question to answer since children come to school with a variety of needs and different levels of experience and skill. Through block accessorizing, teachers can help the children move to higher skill levels.

Using the Activities

There are three levels of difficulty shown with the activities in this book. The first level is **beginning.** Generally speaking, these activities are for ages three-six. The children do the activities themselves with little support from the teacher. However, the teacher will need to introduce some of the activities (a good example is Towers, Buildings, and Skyscrapers on pages 96-97).

The next level is **intermediate,** the middle level of difficulty. These activities require more thinking by the children. For example, look at pages 104-106, Building with Task Cards. The children learn about a variety of structures, and then duplicate what they see on the cards. This activity requires a number of insights. The children must: (1) understand that homes, bridges, and cities are built by people; (2) observe that each of the buildings has different characteristics; (3) know that it is possible to construct a structure, similar to the example, using other materials (accepting a representation of something for the thing itself); (4) move their eyes from a picture on the wall to the work in front of them; and (5) remember the picture and build it. As the difficulty level of the activities increases, the children learn about architecture, symbolic representation, work planning, symmetry, balance, and the roles of people in the work place.

The third difficulty level is **advanced,** requiring more complex thinking by children. These activities will add to children's previous knowledge, and they will use a combination of academic skills. For example, in Changing Block Structures on pages 125-126, children combine patterning and creating change, and they analyze and synthesize what they have learned. The child's chronological age for working at the "advanced" level is not important. What matters is the how he functions in the setting in which he is placed. Is he successful or bored? When you can answer that question, you will know what to do next.

As the year progresses, children need a variety of activities at each difficulty level. The children will move through predictable levels at their own pace. Having choices is essential because they like to work at a comfort level that keeps them challenged, but not anxious. They enjoy taking academic "risks," but only if they have experienced success at a previous level. Even though they may choose the "right" activity for their developmental level, sometimes you will have to urge a child to take on a little more. In an atmosphere of trust, driven by encouragement, a child willingly takes on new challenges.

When you read the activities in this book, keep in mind that these activities are guidelines only. As their teacher, you know the children and how they learn best. Sift and sort through each activity presented in this book to find out what works for you. Take what you need from them and use them. Feel free to modify, revise, or delete the any part of an activity. If you have a better idea, use it! For example, you might decide to introduce or demonstrate a new activity to a small group of children already working in the Block Center (as opposed to the whole class). Let the children show other children what to do when they come to an area to work. Children are the most important aspect of any lesson—the more they do of it, the more they will learn from it.

Think about modeling the behavior that you want the children to emulate. For example, sit in the Block Center and arrange the accessories and the buildings in a new way. Add things.

Task Cards

There are two types of task cards. One type is picture directions, and the other type is a task card made from photographs or magazine pictures of structures.

You can purchase picture direction task cards or make your own. They also are called rebuses and job-work cards. Task cards might say in words and pictures, "Get out the blocks," "Build with the blocks," and "Put the blocks away." The words would be written below drawings of the activity being described. The purpose of the task card is to invite children to work independently by "reading" the directions and working at their own pace.

How to use the Block Center

① Get your blocks.

② Build with your blocks.

③ Put your blocks away.

Commercially made task cards are available through school supply companies, and there are several task-card books on the market. They allow you to copy, color, and display the task cards in your classroom.

You can also draw your own task cards. (I draw my own cards, and the children in my class have never noticed that I am not an artist.) As long as the children can figure out what to do next, they can learn many things independently. If you draw your picture directions, keep the directions simple and the drawing crisp (two-dimensional). The children must be able to focus quickly on the core directions. Add print below each picture. The children "tie" the picture directions to the print. Readers and non-readers can follow the directions at their own pace, at their own level of comfort. Using the task cards lets you offer choices, while encouraging independence.

The second type of task card are those that you make from photographs or magazines pictures of structures such as buildings, sculptures, towers, windmills, and bridges. Glue these pictures to a stiff material, such as cardboard, and place them in the Block Center. They are used to encourage the children to build something similar to what is pictured on the task card. Laminating these task cards extends their life. These task cards are not picture directions, they are idea starters! Famous Paintings, Buildings, and Structures (pages 111-112) is a good example of this kind of a task card.

Below is a list of resources from which to make task cards. Put out a set (10-12) for a week or two in a container in the Block Center, and see what the children do with them. Or introduce one or two task cards to the whole group and refer to "a stack of cards in the Block Center." At other times—especially when the children seem stumped—model using the task cards to make something. It usually gives the children a little nudge. Here is the resource list:

- ✔ calendars with structures as themes
- ✔ tabletop art books of buildings, bridges, and other structures
- ✔ home magazines with photographs of the inside and outside of houses
- ✔ architectural magazines with photographs of famous buildings
- ✔ travel books and brochures
- ✔ school supply catalogs

newspaper

Museum of Texas Handmade Furniture New Braunfels, TX

windmill

Advertisement for a visit to Texas

You are not looking for the children to duplicate the task cards; you are giving the children building ideas—a start!

A Closer Look at the Activities

Some of the activities suggest that you make accessories, or props, to add to block play. These accessories enrich the Block Center and help motivate the children. Some of the props can be used in combination with others, or used separately. What you use depends on the levels of ability of the children in the center at the time. A good example of accessories to make is Bendable Bead People on pages 89-91.

Other activities suggest that you use a "how-to" demonstration (called "With the Children") using the new props or materials in the Block Center. First, describe the prop you are adding and how to use it. Afterward, put it in the center so the children can explore and experiment using the prop. By using this approach, you may also teach the children a few new vocabulary words. Help them use the new words and practice them as they play. A good example of this is Structural Reflections on pages 113-114, where the children learn the words *perspective, reflection,* and *symmetry.* This activity involves the use of Mylar mirrors. They will gain much more from using the mirrors if you demonstrate, explain, and discuss what the new words mean. Children have a greater investment in their own learning when they are a part it from the beginning. As they work with the mirrors, they learn the new vocabulary words—words they would be at a loss to use unless you modeled them and gave them opportunities to practice using them.

Direct teaching is required for some of the more challenging activities. When you challenge the children, you ask them to analyze, generalize, critique, and create. A good example of a direct teaching activity is Words About Blocks on pages 75-76. In this activity, you discuss the characteristics of blocks. The children come up with a list of descriptive words for blocks (for example, square, rectangle, and corner), and you write them down on a chart. Remember, though, descriptive words are abstractions for young children—they don't think of them easily. After you write down the words, post them in their play area. This lets them know that you value their words, and the children will value them as well. Posting their words invariably encourages the "bubbling up" of new descriptive words, such as "hard" and "smooth." Add the new words to the prized list! So jump in when a "bubble up" happens and build on it by asking, "What other words are like that?" These are called "teachable moments." Keep a pencil beside the chart in the Block Center. When the children "bubble," add another word!

You can make the activities that will take more than one day to complete part of a study. Simple Machines on pages 133-135 fits well into a study of either transportation or

Making Connections to New Learning (Or Block Tracks)
69

machines. For example, present a simple machine each day using blocks to introduce the subjects. An in-depth study of machines, however, requires many days. After you model how to make and use a simple machine, the children can show each other. They love to show others what they know.

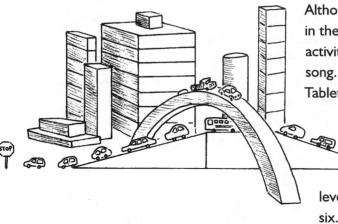

You can also choose an activity to go with a topic your class is learning. You might be doing a study of "Me," for example. In the study, you measure the weight and height of each child. Put Measuring Tools and a Measure Mat (pages 79-81) in the Block Center. These activities will enrich what children are learning by increasing the children's interest in measuring things.

Although it may seem strange, literature belongs in the Block Center, too. Therefore, some of the activities build on literature—a story, poem, or song. A good example of a literature activity is Tabletop Blocks on pages 99-100. In this activity, a poem conveys instructions for building. This kind of activity works well with children in the developmental block stages of five or six—it challenges the level five children and motivates those at level six.

Let me tell you a story about Sara and Steve. (They are not "real" children; I have given them names because they are going to be my examples.) They are like a lot of children I have taught over the years. Steve and Sara loved to write stories in the Library Center, but they never wanted to go to the Block Center. To motivate them to go to the Block Center, I introduced Blocks: Stories About Building on pages 124-125. Initially, they were drawn to the Block Center by an activity they were comfortable with in the Library Center. They started going somewhat tentatively, and began writing there. Guess who they met in the Block Center? Robert! He was building happily with blocks. Pretty soon, Sara and Steve started doing what Robert was doing, and Robert started doing what Sara and Steve were doing. Other children arrived and they began doing the things they observed other children doing successfully. The contagion spread, and the mix of subjects broadened. While the transition may not be smooth and continuous and there may be many fits and starts, it is lots of fun to watch.

What if the Block Center is empty? What do you do? Put a Block Center activity about making a prop into the Art Center. The children will want to use the prop, so this will create interest in the Block Center because the children will want to use their creation. Select an activity, such as the "Stained Glass Window" on page 141-143. Let the children make the stained glass windows in the Art Center, and then use them in the Block Center to build a place to live. If you make the stained glass windows, it should cause a stir because children love to use windows in their buildings. (The tape used in this activity is also a big draw.)

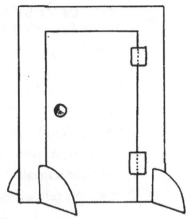

What if the children request a previous activity used in the Block Center? Windows and Doors (on pages 108-111) is an activity that children frequently request throughout the school year. Each time I bring it out, however, the level of play advances. The children are ready to do something new with the windows and doors—they learn to use the same accessories in more complex ways.

Each activity can be adapted to fit the different skill and ability levels of the children in your classroom. If you need simple activities, for example, leave out the more difficult elements of an activity or shorten it. Make a difficult activity simpler by introducing it over several days, rather than trying to do it in one day. To make an activity harder, let the children do some parts of the activity that would normally be done by the teacher.

Remember that while most of the activities in this book were written with unit blocks in mind, you can substitute other construction materials.

In summary, whatever you do, match the choice of activity to the children's developmental level. Make sure they are ready for the shift in focus, to extend themselves and broaden their learning. Let the children guide your actions. What are they doing? Their behavior will tell you when to change things around. When they consistently misuse equipment, or when they don't choose it, they are telling you they are finished with it (at least for now). Put it away and get out something new! Then try putting it out again in six weeks. The children will respond to it like they are seeing an old friend again.

When the children finish an activity, introduce a new one or take a break and resume "ordinary" building. Let the children enjoy their sense of accomplishment. Young children need breaks, and opportunities to "just build stuff" are important.

Let's try some exciting block activities!

Beginning Activities

Working with Blocks Independently

LEVEL: BEGINNING

Social-Emotional Skills: To follow directions independently

Math Skills: To learn one-to-one correspondence

Literacy and Language Arts Skills: To "read" the rebus picture-directions

Materials

Picture directions (see illustration)

Scissors

Construction paper

Unit blocks

Crayons

Glue

Clear contact paper or laminate, optional

How to use the Block Center

① Get your blocks.

② Build with your blocks.

③ Put your blocks away.

With the Children

1. Copy, color, cut out, and glue the picture directions (see illustration) to a sheet of construction paper.
2. Laminate or cover the sheet with clear contact paper, if desired.

Block Center Activity

1. Attach the picture-direction card to a wall in the Block Center at the children's eye level.
2. Talk about the three steps of building with blocks: (1) take the blocks from the shelf, (2) build with them, and (3) put them away.
3. Point to the picture directions frequently as you speak; remind children to use all three steps.
4. The directions are self-instruction tools the children can rely on. Teach to the picture-direction tool, not to the task. For example, ask, "What do the picture directions say?" instead of "Put up the blocks." The first question encourages thought followed by independent action.

Suggestions for Assessment

Photograph the child putting her blocks away, matching the blocks to the silhouettes on the block storage shelves in order from left to right and from top to bottom. Write an anecdotal record describing the child carrying out a task by following the directions.

Partnership Building

LEVEL: BEGINNING

Social-Emotional Skills: To work together

Art Skills: To use creativity (to make something new)

Materials

Two children
Unit blocks
Picture-direction card

With the Children

1. Choose one child to work with.
2. Ask her to gather five blocks for herself and five for you. (With older children, try 10 to 20 blocks for each person.)
3. Explain that you are her partner and the two of you are going to do "partner-

ship building."

4. Put down one block to start a building, and then ask her to put down one of her blocks. Continue taking turns until you both put down all your blocks.

5. Talk about what your blocks or structure look like and ask her to do the same. Choose names for the structures.

6. Take down the structure and put away the blocks. Ask her to do the same.

7. Encourage her to select a classmate and do more partnership building. The other children may have observed the game and may be anxious to play.

① Make a building.

Suggestions for Assessment

Write anecdotal records about the children working together. What are they doing? What do their faces say? Comment on the degree of cooperation, collaboration, helpfulness, and respect one child has for the work of another. Take a photograph of the children working together.

② Get a friend.

③ Tell the friend how to make a building like your building.

Words About Blocks

LEVEL: BEGINNING

Literacy and Language Arts Skills: To develop new vocabulary; to build a sight-word vocabulary

Materials
18" x 24" (45 cm x 60 cm) sheet of paper cut into the shape of a block
Markers
Unit blocks

With the Children
1. Talk about words that describe blocks, such as *corner, edge, tall, hard, flat,* and *round*.
2. Ask the children to help you generate a list of words.
3. Write the words on the block-shaped paper. Beside each block, write the name of the child who contributed the word. The sheet can become the class word chart. Note: Some of the words the children in my class contributed included the names of the structures they made such as castle, barn, and fire station.

Block Center Activity
1. Hang the word chart on a wall in the Block Center at the children's eye level.
2. When a child has built a "tall" building, point to the word *tall* on the chart. When a group builds a "fire station," point to the words *fire station* on the chart.
3. Keep a marker available to add words to the chart. Let the children write the word if possible. Note: Children often will use their own word contributions.

Word Chart

corner.....Jennifer
edge ......Ronnie
tall.........Sam
hard......Caitlin
flat ....Adam
round.....Sophie

When you have moved on to other words, cut out the old words from the word list. Place each word the child contributed in the individual child's portfolio. If a child has "built" her word, take a photograph of it, attach it to the written word, and put it in her portfolio.

Balancing Blocks

LEVEL: BEGINNING

Science Skills: To understand weight and balance of similar and dissimilar objects.

Math Skills: To understand the equivalence of similar and dissimilar objects

Materials
Balance scale
Basket of different shapes and sizes of unit blocks

With the Children
1. Place the basket of blocks and the balance scale so all the children can see it.
2. Put a unit block on one side of the balance scale.
3. Display several blocks on the floor (for example: two triangles, one square, and two columns).
4. Ask the children to guess which of the blocks on the floor, alone or in a combination, will balance the unit block.
5. Encourage them to test their guesses.
6. When the children have discovered which blocks balance the unit block, remove the unit block from the balance scale and set it on the floor with the others.

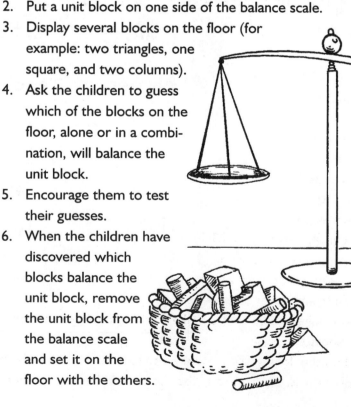

7. On top of the unit block, make another "unit block" by combining other smaller blocks.

     Note: Four small triangles make one unit block. This task teaches children that the blocks are in mathematical proportion.

Block Center Activity

1. Place the balance scale in the Block Center so the children can experiment with the blocks and the balance scale.

Suggestions for Assessment

Write anecdotal records about how children use the balance scale. Are they able to balance dissimilar blocks? Block combinations? Take a photograph of the block configuration when a child assembles a "unit block" by placing smaller blocks on top of a unit block.

How Many Blocks High Am I?

LEVEL: BEGINNING

Math Skills: To understand measurement in terms of blocks (non-standard measurement)

Social-Emotional Skills: To practice adaptive group behaviors

Materials

Unit blocks
Basket
Doll or stuffed animal
Large chart paper
Marker

With the Children

1. Before the children arrive, put 20-25 unit blocks in a basket.
2. Put the basket in the group area.
3. Display the doll so all the children can see it. Ask them, "How many blocks tall is the doll (from her head to her toes)?"
4. Choose two children to go to the basket. Ask each of them to remove the number of blocks she thinks the doll is tall.
5. Lay the doll on the floor. Ask the children to lay the blocks beside the doll. One child uses one side of the doll; the second child uses the other.

Name	Guess	Number of Blocks
Joe	2	7
Carrie	26	6+
Hector	10	8
Ti	4	6

6. How close are the children's guesses? How close is the group guess? Ask the children to add or subtract blocks to get the right count for the doll's height.

7. Then, ask each child to guess how many blocks tall she is and write the guesses on a large piece of chart paper. Write each child's name on the chart, leaving space beside the child's entry so that you can write the correct number (see illustration).

8. After all the children have guessed how tall they are in blocks, write the correct number beside each of their guesses. Explain that you are going to put the chart and a marker in the Block Center for them to measure each other. Leave lots of space on the chart for re-measurements and more re-measurements.

Block Center Activity

1. Hang the chart and a pen at the children's eye level in the Block Center.

Suggestions for Assessment

Cut the chart into sections, keeping a number writing sample for each child. Put the writing samples in each child's portfolio. Observe each child as she works in groups. Write an anecdotal record about how she gets along in group activity. Is she involved or spectating? Does she follow the directions of another child or do her own thing?

The Measure Mat: A "Feet" of Measurement

LEVEL: BEGINNING

Math Skills: To develop an understanding of standard measurement

Literacy and Language Arts Skills: To develop new vocabulary words

Materials

24" (60 cm) ruler
Butcher paper or Pelon (also called interfacing—
    use the non-fusing type)
Black marker
Clear contact paper or laminate, optional
Unit blocks

With the Children

1. Use a 24" (60 cm) ruler to measure a 40" (100 cm) sheet of butcher paper or Pelon.
2. Two inches from one end, draw a straight line halfway across the width of the paper.
3. Write the number "0" above the line.
4. Measure 14" (35 cm) from the same end. Draw a second line. Write the number "1" and the word "foot" above the line.
5. Measure 26" (65 cm) from the same end. Draw a third line. Write the number "2" and the word "feet."
6. Measure 38" (95 cm) from the same end. Draw a fourth line. Write the number "3" and the word "feet" beside it.

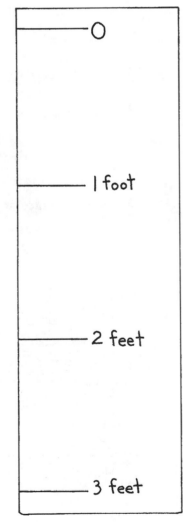

7. If desired, laminate the measure mat or cover it with clear contact paper to extend its useful life.

Block Center Activity
1. Place the measure mat in the Block Center so the children can measure what they build.
2. Show them how to slide it up against a structure or one of their roadways to measure width and length.
3. Many children will say "foots" for "feet" and "feets" for "feet." In time, however, they will learn the singular and plural forms of the word.

Suggestions for Assessment
When a child starts her building at "0" on the measure mat and builds toward the "3" (foot) line two or three times, you will know she has learned something about measurement. Photograph the event and put it in her portfolio. Write anecdotal records when you hear a child add the words "feet" and "foot" to her vocabulary and look for proper usage of the singular and plural when a child uses the words correctly.

Tools for Measurement

LEVEL: BEGINNING

Math Skills: To learn to differentiate length, height, and width

Literacy and Language Arts Skills: To develop new vocabulary, such as *tallest, longest,* and *shortest,* and *taller, shorter,* and *longer*

Materials
Standard measuring tools, such as a tape measure, fold-out tape, retractable tape, ruler, yardstick, protractor, and a level
Non-standard measuring tools, such as adding machine tape, string, Unifix cubes, tongue depressors, and ribbon
Basket
Unit blocks

Block Center Activity

1. Place a few of the standard and non-standard measuring tools in a basket in the Block Center.
2. Encourage the children to use them to measure their block constructions.

Suggestions for Assessment

Take a photograph of the child using the tools to measure her constructions. Add it to her portfolio. Place a tape recorder in the Block Center to record the use of the new words the child is learning.

Pattern Board

LEVEL: BEGINNING

Math Skills: To learn to recognize and describe patterns

Literacy and Language Arts Skills: To learn new vocabulary words, such as *stripe, check, hound's tooth, plaid, zigzag, circular, diagonal,* and other words that describe patterns

Materials

2" (5 cm) clear plastic tape
8" x 10" (20 cm x 25 cm) cardboard pieces (one piece for each fabric sample)
Scissors
Fabric patterns that are easily identified
Glue
Unit blocks

With the Children

1. Tape the pieces of cardboard together using 2" (5 cm) clear plastic tape to make a hinge.
   Note: Tape as many cardboard pieces together as you like; however, hinging together more than three will allow them to stand up freely.
2. Cut fabric to fit the cardboard and glue the pieces to the cardboard. (Covering both sides allows two children to work on it, one on each side of the Pattern Board.) Let the fabric squares dry for several hours.
   Note: If you cannot find fabrics with easy-to-distinguish patterns, draw the designs yourself onto the cardboard.
3. Work with groups of three to four children. Put up a "Closed" sign at the

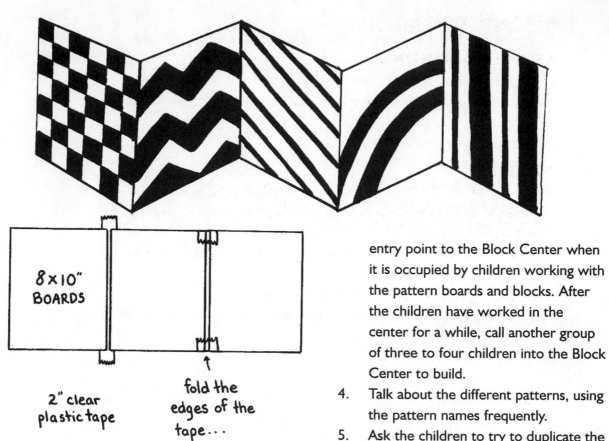

8×10" BOARDS

2" clear plastic tape

fold the edges of the tape...

entry point to the Block Center when it is occupied by children working with the pattern boards and blocks. After the children have worked in the center for a while, call another group of three to four children into the Block Center to build.

4. Talk about the different patterns, using the pattern names frequently.

5. Ask the children to try to duplicate the patterns using the blocks. Discuss how each child, or group of children, replicates a pattern(s).

Block Center Activity

1. Place the Pattern Boards in the Block Center and encourage the children to make similar patterns using unit blocks.

Suggestions for Assessment

Write anecdotal records of your observations of the children working with the Pattern Boards and blocks. Record the names of the children who were able to describe and repeat the patterns with the blocks. Place a tape recorder in the Block Center. Listen for those children who were able to use the new vocabulary words to describe what they were doing with the blocks.

Task Card Display Board

LEVEL: BEGINNING

Physical Development Skills: To develop hand-eye coordination

Materials

Discarded, cardboard fabric bolt (you can usually find these at fabric stores for no charge), or use three pieces of cardboard glued together
Contact paper, any color
Leftover laminating film or acetate sheets (available from art supply stores)
Scissors
Clear packing tape or colored masking tape
Backing from an old stand-up, desktop picture frame (it usually has a cardboard flip-out to stand up the frame)
Glue

With the Children

1. Cover the cardboard bolt with contact paper.
2. Cut two 5" x 11" (12 cm x 27 cm) strips of clear laminating film.
3. Tape the laminating film along the lower edge of the fabric bolt to make pockets for the task cards.
4. To make the display board stand up, glue the picture frame backing to the reverse side of the display board.

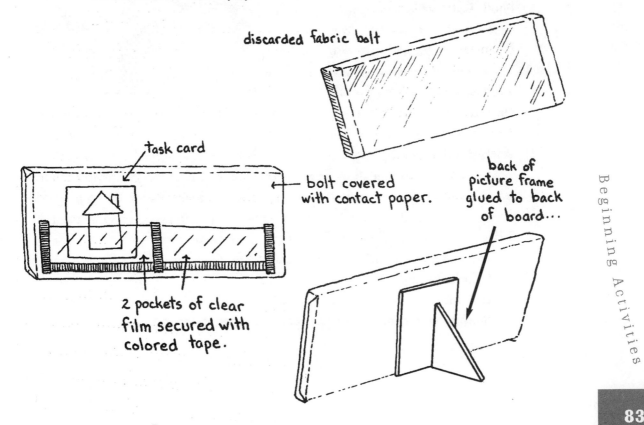

discarded fabric bolt

task card

bolt covered with contact paper.

2 pockets of clear film secured with colored tape.

back of picture frame glued to back of board...

Block Center Activity

1. The task card display board is freestanding when you complete it.
2. The children can use it to stand up their task cards next to their constructions.

Suggestions for Assessment

Take photographs of the children using the task card display board next to their constructions.

Tunnels*

LEVEL: BEGINNING

Physical Development Skills: To develop hand-grasping and pincher control

Math Skills: To learn to make and implement a plan

Materials (select all or some from the list below)

Paper towel or toilet paper cylinders, large fabric cylinders, frozen juice cans (with tops and bottoms removed), PVC pipe [2" or 3" (5 to 7 cm) in diameter and about 6" (15 cm) long]

Contact paper, fabric, foil, or spray paint

Scissors

Photographs of tunnels from magazines

Glue

Construction paper

Clear contact paper or laminate, optional

Small cars

Unit blocks

cut out shaded area.

With the Children

1. Make roadway tunnels by covering cylinders with contact paper, foil, fabric, or spray paint. (Foil is easiest to use, but it tears quickly. Fabric lasts a long time, but you'll need to use fabric glue to adhere it to the cylinder. Spray paint works well, but it is messy. If you use it, cover the work surface thoroughly with newspaper and apply two coats. Contact paper is great, but it is hard to fit on the cylinder.)
2. Cut out photographs of tunnels, glue them to construction paper, and laminate them or cover them with clear contact paper, if desired.

Block Center Activity

1. Place the tunnels in the center along with small cars.
2. Encourage the children to build with blocks, adding tunnels for the cars to go through.
3. Place the tunnel photographs on a Block Center wall at the children's eye level.
4. The children can refer to them as they build with their blocks and tunnels.

Suggestions for Assessment

Take a photograph of the children's efforts to use the tunnel(s). For older children, ask them to draw a picture of how they used the tunnels.

*   Use Tunnels with the New-Block-City Floor Mat (pages 95-96).

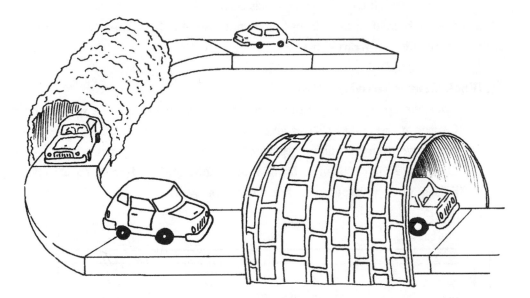

Picture This House

LEVEL: BEGINNING

Science Skills: To learn ways to solve problems

Literacy and Language Arts Skills: To understand that block structures are representations of things, like letters in words represent oral sounds

Materials

Photograph of your house
Glue
Construction paper
Clear contact paper or laminate, optional
Unit blocks
Basket, optional

With the Children

1. Take a color photograph of the outside of your house and get it enlarged.
2. Glue the enlargement to construction paper.
3. If desired, laminate both the enlargement and the original photograph.
4. Display the enlargement and the original photograph of your house. Talk about how it looks and how it was built.
5. Ask each child to talk about her own house. Ask how their houses are similar to or different from yours.

Block Center Activity

1. Place the enlargement of the photograph of your house on a wall of the Block Center at the children's eye level.
2. Challenge them to build a replica of your house with blocks.
3. Encourage the children to bring photographs of their homes to school.
4. Enlarge their photographs as you did your own.

5. Place them on the wall in the Block Center and encourage the children to build replicas of their own houses.
6. Or, put the photographs in a basket. Ask the children to match their photos to the enlarged version of their houses.

Suggestions for Assessment
Write anecdotal records about what the child did in her building effort. What did she say to others about it? What did she say to you? Ask the child to draw a picture of the block structure she built.

Accessorizing the Block Center

LEVEL: BEGINNING

Math Skills: To develop spatial awareness by arranging objects on a surface within a boundary (for example, how far apart, or how close together, should you place related objects to form a "family" of objects); to learn to measure the distances between objects

Literacy and Language Arts Skills: To understand and use representations of things for the things themselves; to develop vocabulary

Materials
Fabric pieces in various sizes and colors
Flashlight
Tulle netting of different colors
Mango wrappings
Unit blocks

Block Center Activity
1. Block Center accessories offer you opportunities to teach across the curriculum. Select accessories that relate to a topic or theme. For example, in the activities suggested below, encourage the children to develop

the math and literacy and language arts skills mentioned above. As the children work with the materials in the ways listed below, you will have opportunities to introduce new vocabulary words such as *heliport, moat,* and *silhouette.*

2. Integrate these accessories, and many others, into the Block Center in a number of ways. Remember to use just a few accessories at a time. Below are some suggestions of how you can use the above materials:

    ✔ Depending on its color, a small piece of fabric can be used to make a lake, a grassy park, a helicopter landing port, a swimming pool, or a tennis court.

    ✔ A large, thin piece of fabric can make a river, a moat around a castle, a trail around a farm, an airport runway, or a bike path in a city park.

    ✔ A flashlight can be used as sunlight, to cast building shadows, and to find hidden things inside buildings.

    ✔ Tulle netting can be draped over structures to create different visual effects, twisted around and trailed from structures, or used to change color.

    ✔ Mango wrappings can be cut and laid out, simulating underground construction, foundation building, and unusual windows in buildings (or, if a child's imagination takes her there, structures erected in outer space).

3. When you add accessories to the Block Center, have a focus in mind. What do you want children to learn? How can the accessories make a specific contribution?

Suggestions for Assessment

Place a tape recorder in the Block Center to record the children's conversation about what they are doing and making with the materials. Write anecdotal records about a child's contribution to the group task or her individual project. Take photographs of the children's use of the materials.

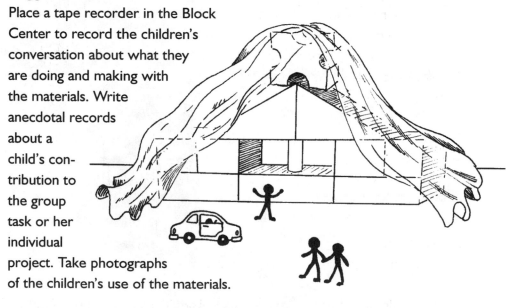

Bendable Bead People*

Literacy and Language Arts Skills: To use oral language in various situations and settings

Physical Development Skills: To encourage and refine eye-hand coordination

Social-Emotional Skills: To act out a role

Materials
Ten ½" or ¾" (1 or 2 cm) wooden beads
Black markers
Colored craft pipe cleaners
Scissors
Hot-glue gun (teacher only)
Basket
Unit blocks

With the Children
1. To make Bendable Bead People, draw a face on a bead with a black marker.
2. Cut one pipe cleaner in half. Keep one half and set the other half aside to make the next bead person.
3. Fold the one-half piece of pipe cleaner in half.
4. Fold a full-length pipe cleaner in half.
5. Twist the half- and the full-length pipe cleaners together at their fold points (see illustration) and push the twisted end through the hole in the bead.
   Note: The twisted ends should protrude slightly from the top of the bead.
6. Squeeze a bit of hot glue into the top bead opening.
7. Unfold the half-length pipe cleaner into arms and the full-length pipe cleaner into legs.

Block Center Activity
1. Place the Bendable Bead People in a basket and put it on a storage shelf in the Block Center.
2. Bendable Bead People make wonderful additions to the Block Center. The children can use the bead people to do imaginary things inside their block structures. The children can place them in and around their structures, simulating and dramatizing the roles of the people who work or live in, or nearby, their block structure.

Suggestions for Assessment

Write anecdotal records about how the children use the bead-people in their play. Photograph the children manipulating the people and talking as they dramatize the everyday lives of the bead people around their structures.

* Special note: Thanks to Dianne Nielsen for this idea!

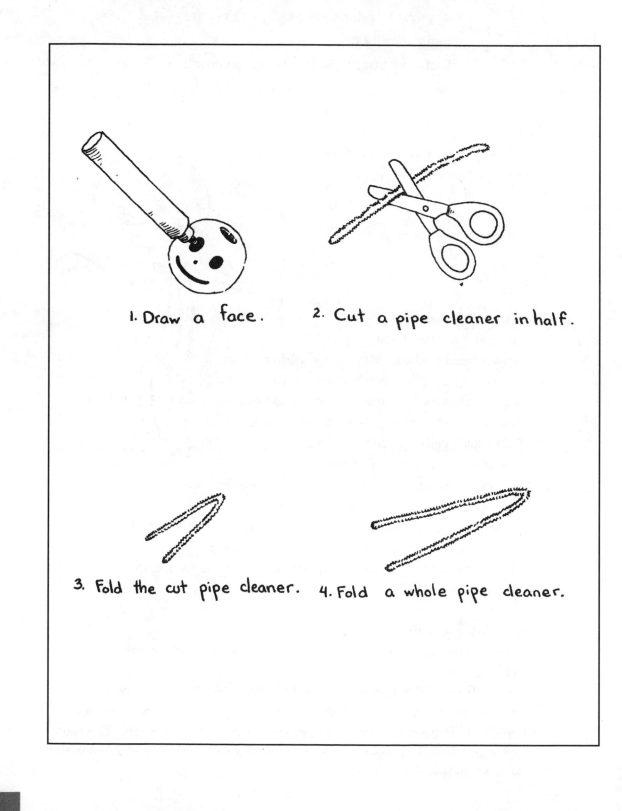

1. Draw a face.

2. Cut a pipe cleaner in half.

3. Fold the cut pipe cleaner.

4. Fold a whole pipe cleaner.

5. Twist the two together.

6. Stick the pipe cleaners into hole.

7. Put hot glue in the hole.

8. Bend the pipe cleaners and make arms and legs!

Craft Board Trees*

LEVEL: BEGINNING

Literacy and Language Arts Skills: To develop oral language; to develop the acceptance of a representation, or a model, of an object for the object itself

Materials

Tree patterns and bases (use the patterns on pages 93-94)

Green craft board (found in craft stores)

Note: When making the tree canopy, use green craft board (with the same color on both sides). If you cannot find craft board, glue two sheets of green poster board together, back-to-back.

Pencil
Matte knife or similar cutting tool (teacher only)
Brown, permanent marker or brown contact paper
Unit blocks

With the Children

1. Enlarge the tree outline (page 93, the Deciduous Tree and Base) and place it on the craft board.
2. Trace the tree and base outline on the craft board and cut it out.
3. Cut the slits that form the base to be joined to the trunk.
4. Color the trunk with the brown marker and draw branches throughout the tree's canopy. If using brown contact paper, cover the trunk with the paper and cut out strips to make branches in the canopy. Do not glue the trees together—you can store them more easily if you take them apart and store them flat.
5. Enlarge the Pine Tree and Base (page 94) and place it on the craft board. Trace and cut out the patterns as you did with the deciduous tree.
6. Since the pine tree has no trunk, cut the slit in the canopy as shown.
7. Cut the slit in the base as you did with the deciduous tree pattern.
8. Attach the base to the canopy.
9. Make several trees for the Block Center. The children can use them for the houses or buildings they erect. If you live in the Southwest and have few trees in your landscape, make a few cacti instead; make patterns and cut them out.

Block Center Activity

1. Place the trees in the Block Center for the children to stand up next to their houses, barns, and fences that they build with blocks.

Suggestions for Assessment

Ask the children to draw pictures of their structures with their trees next to them. Add their drawings to their portfolios. Write an anecdotal record when a child knows that a representation of a tree can easily be accepted for a real one.

* Use craft board trees with the New-Block-City Floor Mat activity (pages 95-96).

Deciduous Tree and Base Pattern

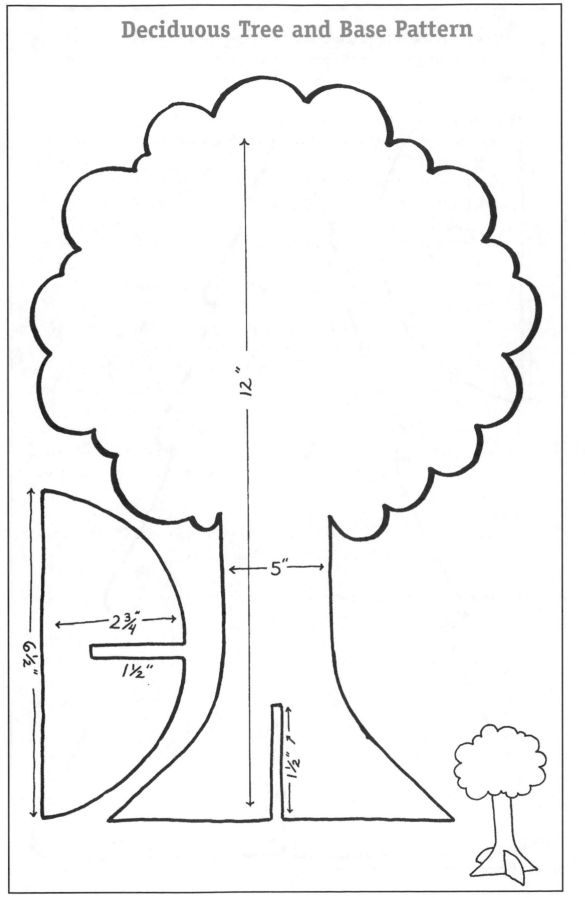

12"

5"

2¾"

1½"

6½"

1½"

Pine Tree and Base Pattern

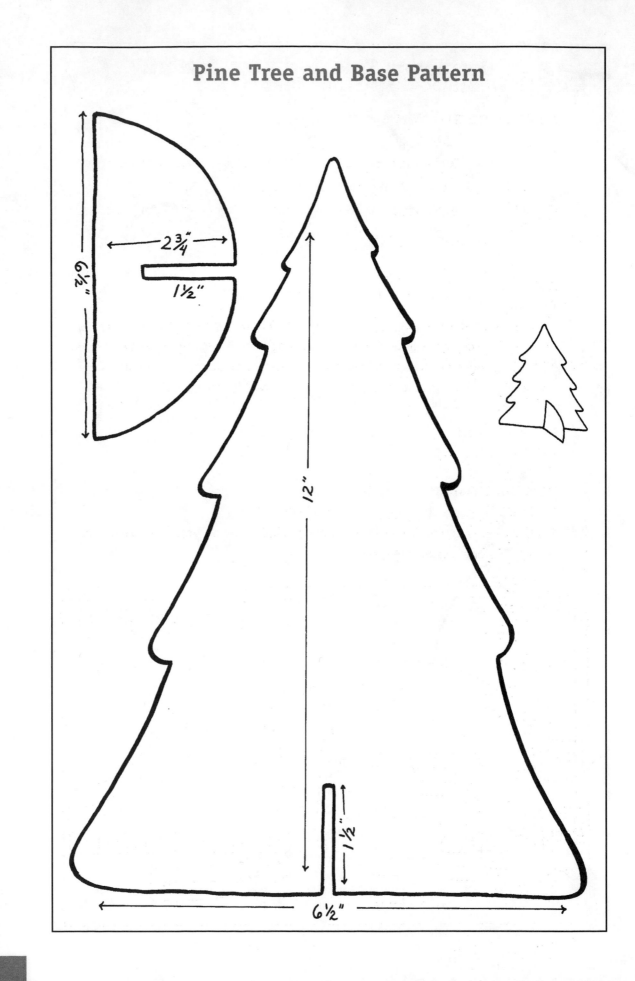

2 3/4"

6 1/2"

1 1/2"

12"

1 1/2"

6 1/2"

The New-Block-City Floor Mat

LEVEL: BEGINNING

Social Skills: To develop an understanding of community, interdependency, and systems

Math Skills: To develop quantitative and spatial skills (how far? how close? how many? and the terms *over, under, around,* and *beside*)

Materials

3'x 5' (1 m x 1.5 m) sheet of green, soft-side Velcro (available in fabric stores)
Hook-side Velcro without peel-and-stick backing (if possible, use white and yellow)
½" (1 cm) pieces of hook-side Velcro with peel-and-stick backing (the amount depends on the size of the floor mat and how it is organized)
Scissors
Blue plastic placemat
Unit blocks

With the Children

1. Place the sheet of green Velcro on the floor.
2. Cut yellow and white, no-peel, sticky-back, hook-side Velcro to create roads and parking lots on the green Velcro mat.

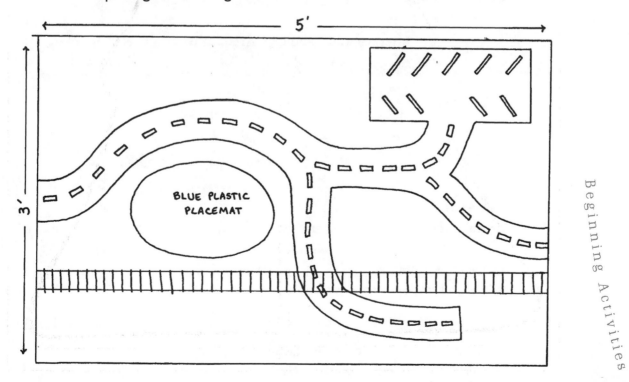

3. Put several pieces of peel-and-stick, hook-side Velcro on the back of a place-mat and place it on the Velcro mat to create a lake. Leave plenty of space to put buildings alongside the road and beside the lake.

Block Center Activity

1. This floor mat makes a defined space for children to build a city, farm, or their community.
2. The children move the roads around on the mat to make different types of communities.
3. If the children would like to use the tunnels (pages 84-85), railroad tracks (pages 138-139), trees (pages 91-94), and towers (pages 96-97), put several pieces of hook-side Velcro with peel-and-stick backing onto the back of the cardboard railroad sheet and the bottom of the tunnels and towers and place them around the mat.

Suggestions for Assessment

Take a photograph of the children's communities to add to their portfolio. Use a tape recorder to capture the children's discussion about their city. Then, make a copy for each child involved in the construction and put it in her portfolio.

Towers, Buildings, and Skyscrapers*

LEVEL: BEGINNING

Literacy and Language Arts Skills: To develop new vocabulary with words such as *tower, skyscraper, elevator, sprinkler,* and *air conditioner*

Math and Science Skills: To develop an understanding of systems, interdependence, patterns, functions, models, representations, and symbols

Materials

Cereal boxes, oatmeal containers, wax paper or aluminum foil boxes, potato chip or tennis ball cans
Aluminum foil (heavy)
Yellow and black permanent markers

With the Children

1. Cover the boxes with heavy aluminum foil, keeping the foil surface as smooth as you can. (Foil is the best material to use because it is easy to repair with tape if damaged.)

2. Draw window outlines with the black permanent marker.

3. Color window spaces with the yellow permanent marker.

Block Center Activity

1. Place the towers, buildings, and skyscrapers in the Block Center.

2. Encourage the children to use them in their construction plans.

Suggestions for Assessment

Write anecdotal records about how the children use the new words introduced by the use of the accessories. Place a tape recorder in the Center; ask the children to talk about their tower. Ask them what people are doing inside their towers.

* Use Towers, Buildings and Skyscrapers with New-Block-City Floor Mat, pages 95-96.

Building Blindfolded

LEVEL: BEGINNING

Physical Skills: To develop body awareness

Math Skills: To learn about size, shape, and weight differences

Note: When children attempt construction activities blindfolded, they develop new parts of their brain to sense size, shape, and proportion. They are able to "see" an object in their head, for example, without seeing it with their eyes. They have to imagine what something looks like and how the parts fit together, which is good practice for having parts of the brain work together to accomplish a task.

Materials

Blindfold (Use a clean cloth to tie around the children's heads or make your own. If you make your own, the materials you need are listed below.)

Scissors

Two small sponges

Elastic thread

Large darning needle

Unit blocks

Basket

With the Children

1. If you are using a cloth, have the children size the fit of the blindfold by putting it on and taking it off by themselves.
2. If you are making your own blindfold, cut the sponges into two 2" to 2 ½" (5 to 6 cm) circles.
3. Use elastic thread and a large darning needle to attach the circles at the point of the nose bridge. Sew the elastic across the opposite edge of the sponges to fit against the back of the head. Make several pairs.
4. Put five or six blocks in a basket. Set the basket in the group area and blindfold one of the children.
5. Ask her to try to build something using all of the blocks in the basket. Ask the class to observe what happens.
6. Talk about how the builder's body is working, even though she cannot see it working.
7. If the child has difficulty in construction, or in using all of the blocks, ask individual class members to offer help. Children's directions about where to move her hand and which block to put on top may be helpful to her. Pick one child at a time to give directions. Move to the next child after one child has offered a direction so all the children will have a turn.
8. When the child has stacked all the blocks, remove the blindfold. Talk about the structure. If there is time, let her revise her structure without a blindfold.
9. Compare the two ways of building.

Block Center Activity

1. Place the blindfold(s) in the Block Center for the children to experience what it is like to build while wearing a blindfold.

Suggestions for Assessment

Observe the children. Write anecdotal records of how they use other parts of their bodies to get the construction job done. Take a photograph of the structure or write a brief description of the activity. If you can, do both and put them in their portfolios.

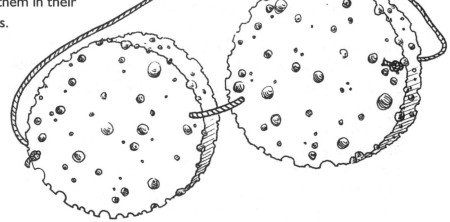

Intermediate Activities

Tabletop Blocks

LEVEL: INTERMEDIATE

Social-Emotional Skills: To work collaboratively and cooperatively with others

Literacy and Language Arts Skills: To use representations of objects and ideas, such as blocks, for the objects or ideas themselves (a higher level skill)

Materials
Groups of 10 unit blocks on trays
Poster-size copy of the poem, "Tabletop Blocks" (see below)

Teacher-Assisted Activity
1. Read "Tabletop Blocks."
2. Discuss the different structures mentioned in the poem. How might the structures look?
3. Divide the class into groups of three to four children.
4. Give each group a tray of blocks and ask each group to work together to erect a castle, town, or barn.
5. When each group is finished building, ask the children to tell you how the poem ends. Let them demonstrate the ending by putting the blocks away.
6. Explain that you will leave the poem in the Block Center and they can build the structures mentioned in the poem.

"Tabletop Blocks" by Sharon MacDonald

Stack the blocks
Up so high.
Very tall
To touch the sky.

Build a castle.
Then, a town.
Make them strong
So they won't fall down.

Build a barn
With straight-up sides
And curvy roads
For tractor rides.

Build a city
With signs that
    show
When to stop
And when to go.

Stack the blocks
On the tray.
It's time to put
Them all away.

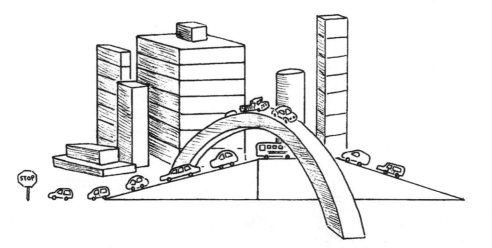

Block Center Activity

1. Make a large poster of the poem so the children can see the words from a distance.
2. Place the poster in the Block Center.
3. The children build a castle, a town with roads, a city, or anything else.

Suggestions for Assessment

Photograph the children working together making their block structures. Write anecdotal records to record that a child can represent objects and ideas with blocks.

Patterns on Adding Machine Tape

LEVEL: INTERMEDIATE

Math Skills: To make and extend patterns, to learn one-to-one correspondence, and to explore shapes

Materials
Adding machine tape
Unit blocks
Black marker
Brown crayon
Scissors
Laminate or clear contact paper, optional
Basket

With the Children
1. Decide on a pattern for the children to match, copy, or extend.
2. Trace different block shapes on adding machine tape in a repeating pattern (for example, rectangle, triangle; rectangle, triangle; and so on). Repeat the pattern several times.
3. Color the block pattern with a brown crayon.
4. Leave space on the adding machine tape to extend the pattern two more times, then cut the tape.
5. Laminate the tape or cover it with clear contact paper, if desired. Roll it up.
6. Trace other patterns onto adding machine tape, extending the pattern of shapes to three (square, rectangle, triangle) and to four (square, rectangle, square, triangle).

Block Center Activity
1. Place the rolls of tape with the block patterns on them in a basket and put them in the Block Center.
2. The children choose a pattern, place the blocks on top of the drawn pattern, and then continue to extend the pattern on the blank part of the tape.
3. To make this activity more challenging, place the tape on the wall for the child to duplicate on the floor.
4. For those children ready to create their own pattern, place a blank roll of adding machine tape, a marker, and a brown crayon in the Block Center.

Suggestions for Assessment

Photograph children extending the existing patterns. Check off "one-to-one cor- respondence" on your developmental checklist when you observe the child matching shapes, correctly putting blocks away, making structures, and filling in the "holes" in the block pattern with blocks.

Maze

LEVEL: INTERMEDIATE

Literacy and Language Arts Skills: To develop new vocabu- lary

Math Skills: To develop mapping skills (the location of objects on a surface); to develop spatial awareness (How far apart can one place things so they still look like a family of things?)

Materials

Unit blocks
One car for each child

With the Children

1. For three days in a row, before the children arrive, make a maze in the Block Center with unit blocks. Make a different maze each day, adding curves and corners, blind alleys, and cul-de-sacs.

2. At group time, make sure that all the children can see the maze you made. Place a car in the maze and ask one child to demonstrate by pushing the car from one point to another inside the maze.

3. Encourage the other children in the group to give directions such as, "Turn at the corner," or "Go straight."

4. Explain that there will be cars in the Block Center and a maze for the children to use during Block Center time. Let them know it is okay for them to make a different maze than the one they start with. Let them take apart the maze and put it back together. Reassembling the maze helps them understand what it is.

Block Center Activity
1. After about three days, the children will understand how a maze works.
2. Encourage them to build their own mazes in the Block Center.
3. Suggest that they challenge other children to push a car through their mazes.

Suggestions for Assessment
Place a tape recorder in the Block Center to record the children using new words when working with mazes. You will pick up lots of side talk about how the maze looks and works. Take photographs of the different mazes the children make, making sure they portray the whole block system that defines the maze. Usually you will see children standing up frequently and looking down at how all the blocks go together. This is especially true if a few children try to make a group maze with a pre-agreed shape or design.

The Chain Reaction

LEVEL: INTERMEDIATE

Science Skills: To understand cause and effect
Math Skills: To recognize a pattern in the placement of the blocks

Materials
Unit blocks
Basket

With the Children
1. Give each child in the group a basic unit block (see illustration, "Unit Block Silhouettes and Names" on page 24).

2. Ask each child to place his block standing on end, in line, one after the other.
3. Encourage the children to space the blocks the right distance apart to cause a chain reaction when someone tips over the first block.
4. After the children have placed all their blocks in a line, ask them to predict what will happen if the first block is pushed against the second.
5. After each child has made a prediction, ask one of the children to push over the first block. Were their predictions correct? What happened? Why?

Block Center Activity

1. Place the basic unit blocks in a basket in the center so the children can use them to play the chain-reaction game.
2. After the children have explored and experimented with the activity, encourage them to return the blocks to the shelf.

Suggestions for Assessment

Keep a written record of each child's predictions and add it to his portfolio. Photograph the child setting up the chain reaction. Look for the spaces between the blocks. Are they close enough together for one to strike the next, yet far enough apart to generate the force needed to push over the next block? Is there an understanding of how the chain reaction works?

Building with Task Cards

LEVEL: INTERMEDIATE

Literacy and Language Arts Skills: To plan a construction; to follow a plan

Art Skills: To develop design ideas; to identify symmetry, not only in the settings in which they live, but in themselves, others, and systems within their environments

Note: Symmetry refers to the natural balance of creatures, objects, words, and systems. For example, how commonplace opposite pairs are in the natural world, like eyes or hands and feet

Materials

Home and travel magazines and travel brochures (especially in European settings)
Early childhood teacher supply catalogs
Scissors

Glue

Construction paper or card stock paper

Clear contact paper or laminate, optional

Basket, optional

With the Children

1. Collect photographs of each of the topics below from magazines and brochures:
   - ✔ Interesting land formations
   - ✔ Unusual bridges
   - ✔ Different styles of homes
   - ✔ Constructions built by children
   - ✔ City skylines
   - ✔ Railroads
   - ✔ A variety of tunnels for cars and trains

2. Cut out the larger photographs and glue them on one size of card stock or construction paper to make task cards. (Using only one size of paper will make storage easier.)

3. Laminate the task cards or cover them with clear contact paper, if desired.

4. Also make task cards using photographs from school supply catalogs. Many photographs show children building with different construction materials that are available.

5. When the children are in a group, show them several of the photographs from magazines and brochures. Talk about them.

6. Then, add the photographs of the structures that other children built from other materials (taken from the school supply catalogs mentioned above).

7. Talk about how the structures are alike and different.
   Note: One day in class we were looking at a photograph of the Golden Gate Bridge spanning the San Francisco Bay. Next to it I had placed a photograph of a bridge, taken from a school supply catalog.

The photograph showed a bridge built by a child using Legos. One child in my class commented on what was alike and different about the two. He remarked: "Big people just have bigger toys to build with...." The rest of my class of four-year-olds nodded soberly. I could barely contain my laughter.

Block Center Activity

1. Display the task cards on a wall in the Block Center or in a basket on a shelf. There are drawbacks to either choice. Consider making a Task Card Display Board (see pages 83-84).
2. Put out a few task cards at a time (using more can be confusing). Change them often.
3. Put the cards out by topic so the children can talk about what is alike and different in one topic at a time. For example, put out bridge task cards. What is alike or different about bridges? Put out skyline task cards. What is alike and different?

   Note: I suggest that you only put out task cards of what adults have built, rather than a mixture of adult and children's work. It invites unnecessary comparisons of young children's work to what typically is quite complex adult work. Use the school supply catalog structures only when introducing an exercise inviting exploration of similarities and differences.

Suggestions for Assessment

Take a photograph of the child's constructions as "likenesses" of the task card he used. Ask the child to draw a picture of his structure and tell you how it compares to the task card.

Columns

LEVEL: INTERMEDIATE

Math Skills: To learn to make and implement a plan; to make probability estimates

Motor Skills Development: To develop small muscles by grasping, moving, and arranging the columns in conjunction with the blocks

Materials

Magazine photographs that show columns as a building feature
Scissors
Glue

Construction paper

Clear contact paper or laminate, optional

Several 4" (10 cm) and 6" (15 cm) columns (Purchase clear or white columns wherever cake-decorating items are sold.)

Unit blocks

With the Children

1. Cut out magazine photographs, glue them to construction paper, and laminate or cover them with clear contact paper (if desired).

2. Before the children arrive, build a small building in the Block Center using front-supporting columns similar to the ones in the photographs.

3. As the children arrive, point out the building and introduce the word *column*. Talk about what a column does. (It is a decoration that also helps hold up parts of the building; it is used inside or outside of a building.)

4. Invite the children to make their own buildings with columns using the ones you have put in the center.

Block Center Activity

1. Place different-length columns and the photographs of buildings with columns in the Block Center.

2. Invite the children to build with the columns.

After backing photos with construction paper, laminate.

Suggestions for Assessment

Tape record a discussion about the sizes of the columns in relation to the size to the blocks they support. Write anecdotal records about the child's ability to bridge the various spans between the blocks and columns in his construction. What did he learn? Are his initial estimates accurate? What did he try?

Windows and Doors

LEVEL: INTERMEDIATE

Math Skills: To develop math-based vocabulary (such as: how far? how close? how many? how much less? in what direction?)

Literacy and Language Arts Skills: To represent a thought, object, or idea as a symbol or as a representation of something, rather than the thing itself

Materials

Matte board (or use craft board, two pieces of poster board, or cardboard covered with contact paper)

X-acto knife or sharp scissors (teacher only)

Marker

Tape

Photographs showing windows and doors in the interiors of houses, backed with construction paper and laminated, optional

With the Children

1. To make four windows, use four pieces of matte board, each 9" x 13" (22 cm x 32 cm). Using an X-acto knife or sharp scissors, cut the windows as shown in the illustration. Start in the upper left corner of the board, 2 ½" (6 cm) from the left edge and 2" (5 cm) from the top. Cut each window 4" (10 cm) wide and 3" (7 cm) high, to make four windowpanes separated by a ½" (1 cm) border.

2. Cut two slits in the bottom of each window, about 2 ½" (6 cm) from each end. (This is where you will insert the bases to allow each window to stand freely). When you are through, you will have four freestanding windows.

3. To make four doors, use four pieces of matte board, each 9" x 13" (22 cm x 32 cm). Cut the doors as shown in the illustration. Start in the upper left corner, 2" (5 cm) from the left edge and 2" (5 cm) from the top. Cut each door opening 5" wide and 11" (12 cm x 27 cm) high.

4. Use a marker to draw a doorknob just above the vertical center of each door, toward the left or right edge of each door.

5. Remove the door from the matte board, then re-insert it and tape it to the side of the door opening, allowing it to swing inward and outward.

6. Cut two slits in the bottom of each door, about 1" (2 cm) from the outside edge, to insert the bases that will allow the door to stand freely. When you are through, you will have four freestanding doors.

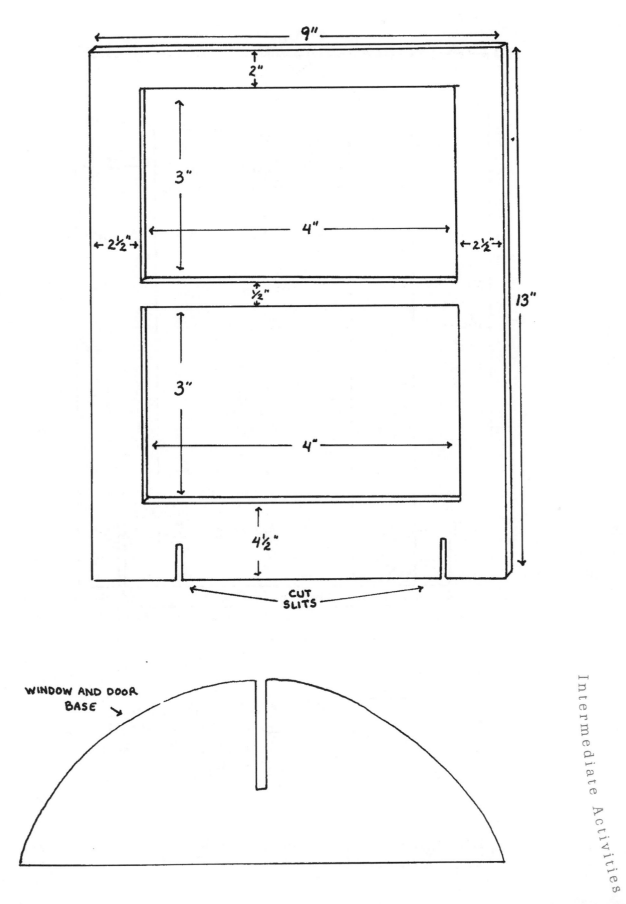

9"

2"

3"

4"

2½"   2½"

½"

3"

4"

13"

4½"

CUT
SLITS

WINDOW AND DOOR
BASE

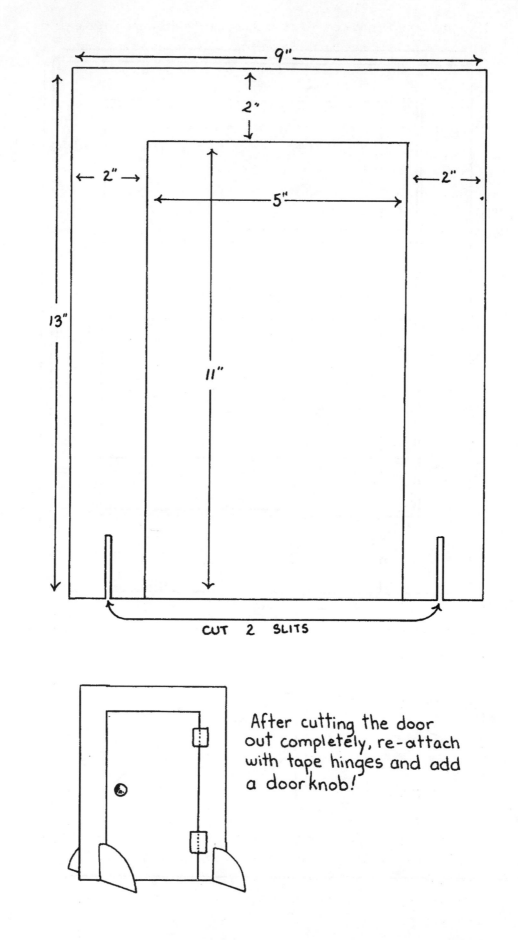

CUT 2 SLITS

After cutting the door
out completely, re-attach
with tape hinges and add
a doorknob!

7. Make the window and door bases as shown in the illustration. Make eight sets, or 16 bases. Insert them into the slits in the windows and doors.

Block Center Activity
1. Place the doors and windows in the Block Center.
2. Encourage the children to build their structures around them.
3. If you have photographs of home interiors, tape them up on the walls for the children to get ideas.

Suggestions for Assessment
Observe the children as they work with the doors and windows. Write anecdotal records about how the children use them. Tape record, for example, the children's discussions about the window placements, and the use of math vocabulary words such as, "How far (over)?" "How much (closer)?" and "Which way (in what direction)?"

Famous Paintings, Buildings, and Structures

LEVEL: INTERMEDIATE

Math Skills: To learn size and shape differentiation
Social-Emotional Skills: To develop respect for the work of others
Art Skills: To investigate various styles in the visual arts

Materials:
Art book of Old Masters' paintings, with subjects that include buildings and other structures
Scissors
Glue
Construction paper
Clear contact paper or laminate, optional
Basket
Unit blocks

With the Children
1. From an art book of Old Masters' paintings, select and make copies of photographs that include people, buildings, farms, and other structures.
2. Make task cards by cutting out the photographs, gluing them to construction paper, and laminating them or covering them with clear contact paper (if desired).

Block Center Activity

1. Place the task cards in a basket and put the basket in the Block Center.
2. Ask children to make structures similar to those in the task cards.
3. Encourage them to refer to the cards frequently to get them started. Discuss how many Old Master artists painted exactly what they saw around them as they went about their daily lives: beautiful churches, elegant castles, grand canals, spreading farms, and buildings bustling with people.

Suggestions for Assessment

Photograph the child's structure with the task card next to it to show his grasp of shape and size and project comprehension. As you discuss the famous artists' buildings with the children, make anecdotal records of the individual child's thoughts and feelings about the building and other structures rendered in the artists' work.

Structural Reflections

LEVEL: INTERMEDIATE

Science Skills: To understand cause and effect

Literacy and Language Arts Skills: To develop new vocabulary

Materials

Small containers, each with six different-shaped unit blocks, one for each group

3"x 6" (7 cm x 15 cm) Mylar sheets, one for each group

Pen

Large sheet of paper

8"x 10" (20 cm x 25 cm) Mylar sheet (fits a standard picture-frame) in a 8"x 10"x 2" (20 cm x 25 cm x 5 cm) clear acrylic, freestanding picture frame

Block Center Activity

1. Divide the class into groups of three or four children.
2. Pass out a container of unit blocks and a 3" x 6" (7 cm x 15 cm) Mylar sheet to each group.
3. Ask the children in each group to work together to build a structure.
4. After they have completed it, ask them hold up the Mylar sheet next to the structure (the structure will be reflected on the Mylar sheet).

5. The children can move around the Mylar sheet to capture a view they like.

6. Discuss what happens to the structure when they move the Mylar sheet. Is the structure itself changed? What changes?

7. Make a list of subjects, ideas, and words about the children's experience. Introduce the words *perspective* (view), *symmetry,* and *reflection* and discuss what each word means. Show the group the 8" x 10" (20 cm x 25 cm) Mylar sheet in the clear acrylic frame.

8. Explain that it will be in the Block Center for them to use to examine the larger structures they build, along with small Mylar sheets for them to use with smaller constructions.

Suggestions for Assessment

Take photographs showing the children using the Mylar sheets to look at the different views (perspectives) of their structures. Tape record the new words the children use to describe what they have seen and learned.

Moonscapes

LEVEL: INTERMEDIATE

Literacy and Language Arts Skills: To learn to develop and implement a plan

Math Skills: To develop spatial awareness by arranging objects on a surface (For example, how far apart, or how close together, do objects need to be for them to relate?)

Materials
Paper towel cylinder
Aluminum foil
Scissors
Poster board or cardboard
Stapler
Glue
Photographs of astronauts and other activities on the moon's surface, laminated to make them into task cards, optional
Basket

With the Children
1. Cover a paper towel cylinder with foil.

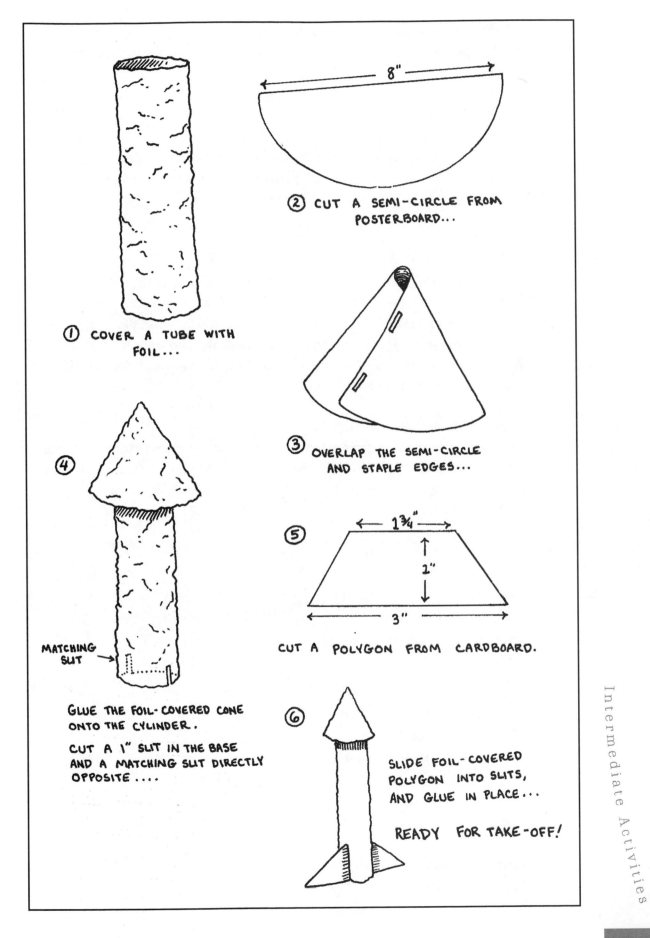

① COVER A TUBE WITH FOIL...

② CUT A SEMI-CIRCLE FROM POSTERBOARD...

8"

③ OVERLAP THE SEMI-CIRCLE AND STAPLE EDGES...

④ MATCHING SLIT

GLUE THE FOIL-COVERED CONE ONTO THE CYLINDER.

CUT A 1" SLIT IN THE BASE AND A MATCHING SLIT DIRECTLY OPPOSITE....

⑤ CUT A POLYGON FROM CARDBOARD.

1¾"

1"

3"

⑥ SLIDE FOIL-COVERED POLYGON INTO SLITS, AND GLUE IN PLACE...

READY FOR TAKE-OFF!

2. Cut a piece of poster board or cardboard into a semi-circle, 8" (20 cm) in diameter. Bend it into the shape of a cone. Overlap the edges and staple them in place.
3. Cover it with foil. Glue the cone to top of the cylinder.
4. To make a rocket stand, cut out a polygon from the cardboard 3" (7 cm) across the base, 1" (2 cm) high, and 1 ¾" (4 cm) across the top (see illustration). Cover it with foil. On the paper-towel cylinder, cut a 1" (2 cm) slit at the base (of the rocket) and on opposite sides. Slide the stand into the slits, and glue it into place as shown in the illustration.

Block Center Activity
1. Place all of the moon accessories—silver lamé fabric for the moon's surface, packing corners covered with foil for the moon's mountains, and small rocks covered with foil—in a basket in the Block Center.
2. Hang photographs of the moon's surface on the wall or use the Task Card Display Board (pages 83-84) to display a particular photograph.
3. The children can use the accessories to make moonscapes from the photographs or from their imaginations.

Suggestions for Assessment
Take photographs of the children's moonscapes and put them in their portfolios, showing that they can implement a plan. Ask the children to write a story about their moonscape. Look to see if the children have a beginning, middle, and an end to their story. Does the story show an understanding of a moonscape?

Estimations and Predictions

LEVEL: INTERMEDIATE

Science Skills: To learn to make predictions and estimates based on observation, then validating or checking the results

Math Skills: To do oral counts; to learn one-to-one correspondence

Materials
20 unit blocks
Wagon or basket
Shoeboxes that are the same size
Sheet of brown construction paper about 24" x 36" (60 cm x 90 cm), cut in the shape of a unit block

Marker

Number line

With the Children

1. Before the children arrive, put out about 20 unit blocks in a wagon or basket and the shoeboxes in the group area.

2. After the children arrive, ask them to estimate how many unit blocks will fit in a shoebox under the following four conditions: (1) standing the blocks up; (2) laying them down flat; (3) laying them on their side; and, (4) piled-up in a big heap.

3. Record their guesses on the block-shaped construction paper sheet, then put out the number line.

4. Ask them to verify their prediction by putting the blocks along the number line. Make a note on the construction paper of the number of blocks used for each condition. What is the best way to get the most blocks in a shoebox?

Block Center Activity

1. Put out the shoeboxes, the blocks, and the number line in the Block Center.

2. Ask the children to make their estimates before they begin to fill the box. Then, they can fill the box.

3. They can verify the accuracy of their estimates by taking the blocks out of the shoebox and setting them beside the number line. Older children can write their guesses on paper, then verify them.

Suggestions for Assessment

Write anecdotal records of your observations of the children working. For example, who makes an estimate before filling the shoebox? Whose guess is close to his original estimate? Who uses the number line? Who counts the blocks as he puts them in the shoebox?

Window Shade Grid

LEVEL: INTERMEDIATE

Math Skills: To learn and apply graphing techniques; to form groups from individual objects that have a common characteristic(s) (For example, when graphing, children will find all the triangles, all the rectangles, and all the cylinders.)

Materials:

24" x 36" (60 cm x 90 cm) window shade—typically the width is the first number
   (If you don't have a window shade, make a grid on construction paper.)
Pencil
Black marker
Yardstick
Unit blocks
Basket

With the Children

1. Lay out a grid on a window shade of 5 ½" (14 cm) squares, using a pencil to make the gridlines. [Note: A unit block is 5 ½" x 2 ¾" (14 cm x 7cm)]. Then, make permanent grid lines using a black marker. Depending on the width of the shade, you will have four to five squares.

2. Before the children arrive, gather different kinds of blocks, making sure you have a different amount of each kind of block. For example, have four triangles, three rectangular unit blocks, and five square blocks. Put all the blocks in the basket.

3. Put the basket and the window shade grid near the group area.

4. When the children arrive, ask them to put a different block in each of the squares along the bottom edge of the window shade grid. Explain that you are going to make a graph of the blocks in the basket.

5. Let each child choose a block to place on the grid, matching the ones that are along the bottom.

6. Discuss how many of each type of blocks there are, and what features or characteristics of each block were used to separate one kind block from another.

Block Center Activity

1. Place the window shade grid in the Block Center for children to use to graph blocks and other construction materials they use.

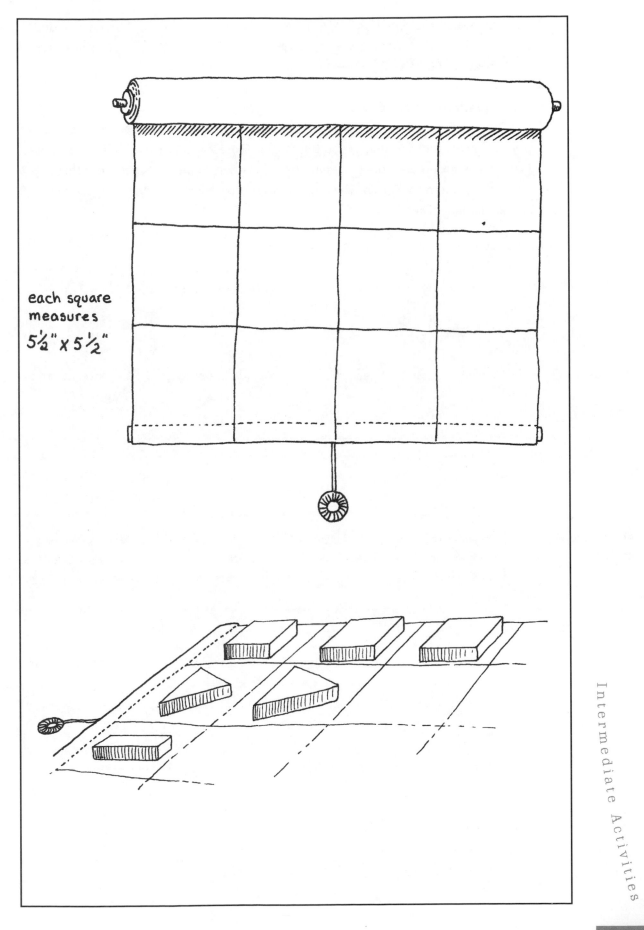

each square measures 5½" x 5½"

2. When they graph, they can answer the following questions: How many kinds of blocks do I use? How many of each kind of block do I use? How are they alike and different?

Suggestions for Assessment

Take a photograph of the children's attempts to graph. Write anecdotal records of your observations as they group the blocks. Expect inconsistencies. For example, they may group both the long- and the short-triangle blocks together. If that happens, ask them to explain why they put them together and what they see that makes them alike.

Advanced Activities

A Story of a Boy and His Blocks

LEVEL: ADVANCED

Thinking Skills: To think creatively

Social-Emotional Skills: To develop problem-solving methods

Literacy and Language Arts Skills: To understand "story-ness" and story sequence (beginning, middle, end)

Materials

"A Story of a Boy and His Blocks" and a copy of the Block Shapes page
   (see page 123)
Brown crayon
Clear contact paper or laminate, optional
Scissors
Sandpaper
Glue
Large, flannel board
One-gallon, resealable plastic bag or container

With the Children

1. Refer to the Block shapes Page (page 123). It shows block shapes that you can "build" or assemble on a flat surface. The forms represent two-dimensional "blocks." Copy it several times.
2. Color the shapes on the copies using a brown crayon.
3. Laminate the pages or cover them with clear contact paper, if desired.
4. Cut out the shapes.
5. Cut out a strip of sandpaper for each block shape and glue each strip to the backs of each shape. The sandpaper will let you stick the shape to the flannel board. Store the pieces in a resealable bag or a small container.
6. Read the first part of the story and make a two-dimensional structure. Talk about what you are doing with the shapes.
7. Read a bit more and ask one or two children to make a structure. This introduction will expose the children to building with blocks in a two-dimensional plane. This is a simpler process and is different than building with blocks in the Block Center.

Block Center Activity

1. Children who do not choose to play in the Block Center often may prefer books. This activity will help them learn about block construction.
2. Place the flannel board and "A Story of a Boy and His Blocks" with the block shapes in the Library Center. After the children listen to the story, they can build the two-dimensional structures using the paper block shapes.

Suggestions for Assessment

Photograph the structures the children "built" with the paper block shapes. The photographs will record the extent to which the child is using her creative thinking. Interview the child on tape about what she has built and the steps she took to build it—capture her story.

A Story of a Boy and His Blocks

Brad was a builder of things. He used lots of different things to build with; like wood pieces, bricks, stones, tree branches, and dirt clods. On rainy days, he took the pillows off the sofa and used them for building. Brad made all kinds of structures with all kinds of things. He was a builder.

Brad was going to be five. A big day! At his birthday party, he opened his gift from his mom and dad. It was a set of wooden blocks. He was so excited he almost fell into the box. He could hardly wait for his party to be over so he could build. And build he did, from that day on!

He built bridges, skyscrapers, and schools. And, he always built streets to connect one place to another. Cars could drive on them.

He liked to build farms and barns, with fences all around. Brad always built a road on the farm, so the farmer could drive his tractor around the farm.

Sometimes Brad would build small things, like a doghouse or a stop sign. Big things interested Brad most though, like a zoo with a park beside, or a city with stores and houses, churches, and hotels. Even an observatory, so people could look at the stars at night through a telescope.

When Brad built a city, he would leave it up for days at a time. He would put a sign by his city saying, "Under Construction! Do not knock my buildings down!"

But sometimes his city buildings would come crashing down. That was okay. Brad pretended that there had been an earthquake or a hurricane. He would start all over again. He was a builder!

When Brad did take down all his blocks, he carefully put them all away. That way, they would all be ready for Brad's next adventure. Brad was a builder!

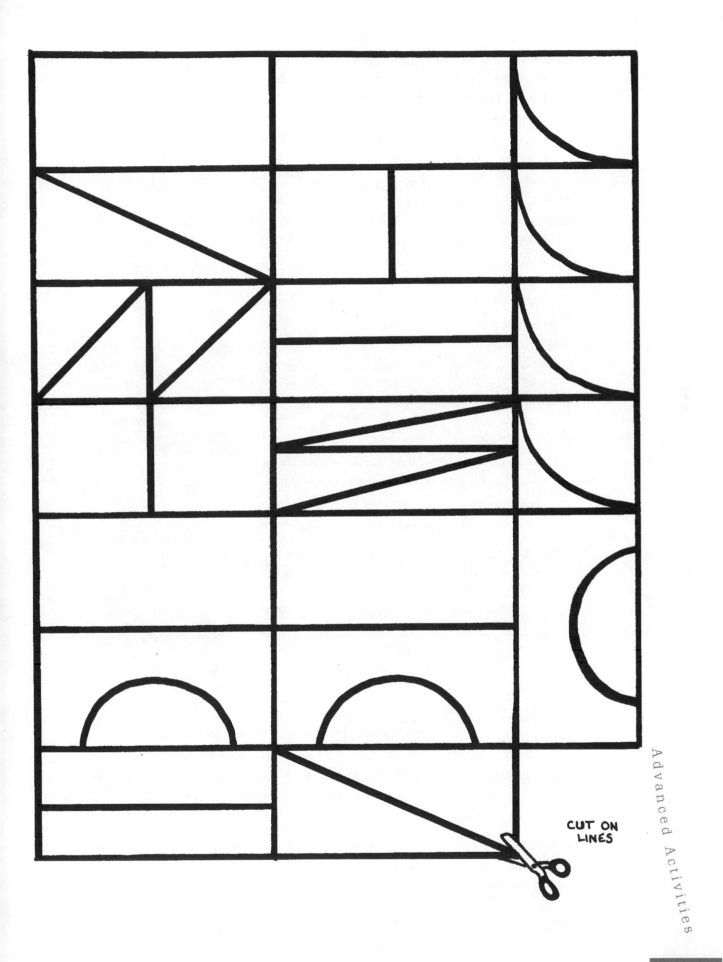

CUT ON
LINES

Blocks: Stories About Building

LEVEL: ADVANCED

Literacy and Language Arts Skills: To accept a representation (such as a block or a word) for the object or idea itself
Physical Development: To develop pincher control when using a pencil

Materials
Brown construction paper
White paper
Stapler
Pencils
Black marker
Small containers of blocks, one container for two children
Large sheet of white paper

With the Children
1. Cut out block shapes from brown construction paper to make blank storybook covers.
2. Using the cutout block shapes as templates, cut out three or four shapes from the sheets of white paper.
3. Staple the white sheets between the brown construction paper covers to make blank block books.
4. To get the children excited about writing stories about their block building, pass out small containers of blocks, one for each pair of children.
5. Give them time to build a structure with the blocks.

6. After they have built their structures, ask each pair of children to describe the construction process. What did they build?
7. Make a word list of what the children say on the large sheet of white paper.
8. Show the children the blank storybooks. Explain that you will put the blank books and the Block Building Word List in the Block Center so they can create their own block story.

Block Center Activity
1. Place the books and pencils in the Block Center.
2. Attach the Block Building Word List to a wall in the center.
3. The children use the blank books to create stories about their building process or their finished structures.

4. The words on the wall can help them write block words in their books.

Suggestions for Assessment
Keep copies of the children's' stories to document that she can use words to represent an idea or thought. Ask the child to read the story and record it using a tape recorder.

Changing Block Structures

LEVEL: ADVANCED

Math Skills: To form new patterns and groups

Science Skills: To recognize and make change in the environment

Materials
Changes, Changes by Pat Hutchins
Tracing paper
Pen
Crayons
Scissors
Construction paper
Glue
Laminate or clear contact paper, optional
Unit blocks

With the Children
1. *Changes, Changes* is a book with pictures of block structures. There are no words. It is a great book to read through, making up stories and explanations of the changes that are taking place as you turn the pages.
2. To make task cards from the book, trace six or seven block structures from the pages.
3. Color them, cut them out, and glue them to construction paper.
4. To extend the useful life of the task cards, cover them with clear contact paper or laminate them, if desired.
5. The first time you go through the book, do it with the children. Encourage them to create a story dialogue as you turn the pages. Talk about how the block structures change in the story and how new structures appear. What happens?
6. Show the children the task cards from the book. Help them find the page in the story that corresponds to each task card.

7. Let the children know that *Changes, Changes* will be in the Block Center for their use. It will help them to build the different structures in the story.

Block Center Activity
1. Place the book and the task cards in the Block Center.
2. Ask the children to use either the book or the task cards to retell what happens as their block structures change over time.
3. They can duplicate the task cards when building with the blocks, or make up their own story about the blocks as they change.

Suggestions for Assessment
Photograph the children as they erect and modify their structures and work with the task cards as they build. Record a sequence of structural changes with photographs. Gather work samples as the children draw their block-change story.

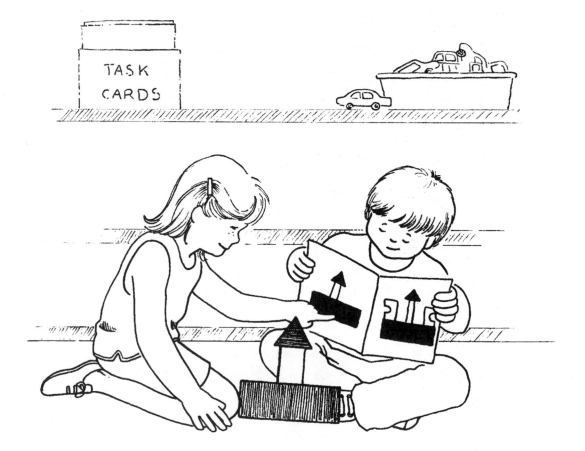

The Three Billy Goats Gruff

LEVEL: ADVANCED

Math Skills: To learn to work with part and whole relationships

Literacy and Language Arts Skills: To learn to retell a story

Materials

Any version of *The Three Billy Goats Gruff*

Goats, in three sizes (see the directions below)

Troll (see the directions below)

Crayons or markers

Scissors

Clear contact paper or laminate, optional

Tape

Unit blocks

Craft board trees (see pages 91-94)

Wide piece of blue ribbon

With the Children

1. Photocopy each of the three goats and the troll.

2. Color the goats and troll and cut them out.

3. Laminate them or cover them with clear contact paper, if desired.

4. Tape the figures to a small block so that the block can stand freely and the figures look like they are standing upright.

5. Before the children arrive, prepare four or five (depending on the number of children in your class) small groups of blocks consisting of two small triangles and one arch.

6. Read *The Three Billy Goats Gruff*. Talk about the story setting depicted in each drawing, as well as the bridge that is pictured in the story. Discuss the

purpose of a bridge—how it is unique in its structure and purpose. If possible, display photographs of other bridges, both man-made and natural. Examine what the bridges are spanning and how the bridges are alike and different.

7. Divide the children into groups of three to four children. Give each group the three blocks described in Step 5. Ask the groups to experiment and try to build a bridge using only the three blocks.

8. If desired, read several versions of the story and ask the children to compare them by describing their likenesses and differences. Then build the story set from each story with the blocks, and compare them as you compared the stories.

Block Center Activity

1. Display the troll and the three goats and explain to the children that they can build bridges in the block area and retell the story.

2. Place trees (see pages 91-94) and a wide piece of blue ribbon (to represent a river) in the Block Center for the children to use when building their bridges.

Suggestions for Assessment

Take photographs as the children use the blocks to make a bridge (they are working with part and whole relationships). Make a tape recording of children retelling the story of *The Three Billy Goats Gruff*.

Phoebe's Block Poem*

LEVEL: ADVANCED

Literacy and Language Arts Skills: To develop word recognition; to recognize rhyming words

Materials
"Phoebe's Poem" (see next page)
18" x 24" (45 cm x 60 cm) piece of poster board
Markers
Hole punch
Brad
3" x 5" (7 cm x 12 cm) unlined index cards
Clear contact paper or laminate, optional
Unit blocks
Two baskets

With the Children
1. Copy "Phoebe's Poem" onto a sheet of poster board.
2. Above the blank space in the first line of the poem, punch a small hole through the poster board.
3. Insert a brad so that the head of the brad is on the reverse side of the poster board, with the two prongs extending through the front of the board.
4. Fold down one of the prongs; fold up the second prong and shape it into a hook.
5. Write the following words on the index cards: *tower, castle, house, building, rocket, fort, ship, skyscraper, town, farm, zoo,* and *cabin.*
6. Laminate (if desired) and punch a hole into the top of each card.
7. Punch a hole into each of the blank index cards; also laminate them if desired.
8. Read "Phoebe's Poem" to a group of three to four children.
9. Give them about eight to ten blocks. Ask them to work together to build a tower (a word on one of the index cards).
10. After they build their tower, show them the word "tower" on the index card.
11. Affix the card to the brad over the blank space on the poster board.
12. Next, ask them to build a

a _____ So high

farm

house from the blocks. After they have built it, replace the word "tower" with the word "house" and attach it to the poster board.

13. Once the children understand the activity (building the different words on the index cards), give them blank laminated cards and let them write their own words to build. Explain that they can build whatever they want. Write the name of what they build on the blank index card and attach it to the brad in the blank space.

14. Repeat the activity with another group of three to four children.

Phoebe's Poem

My blocks go up a _____ so high
They almost reach to the sky.
Now see them fall upon the floor,
So I can build them up once more.
Up and down, up and down,
See my blocks go up and down!

Block Center Activity

1. Hang the poem on a wall in the Block Center.
2. Put the index cards in a basket on a shelf.
3. Place the blank, laminated index cards and a marker in a second basket. The

---

PHOEBE'S POEM

My blocks go up a _____ so high
They almost reach to the sky.

Now see them fall upon the floor,
   So I can build them up once more.

Up and down, up and down,
   See my blocks go up and down!

children can use either the pre-made index card words, or after deciding what to build, they can write their new words on the index card.

Suggestions for Assessment

If the children make their own index cards, save them and put them in each of their portfolios. Write anecdotal records of the words the children are able to read.

* A special thanks to Phoebe Ingram for letting me use her poem.

The Do-Nothing Machine

LEVEL: ADVANCED

Literacy and Language Arts Skills: To recognize rhyming words

Science Skills: To think about structures in new ways, then to make plans to construct them

Materials

The "Do-Nothing Machine" poem (see next page)

Basket

Assorted materials, such as string, paper or plastic letters, beads, colored phone-cable wire (these are multi-colored wires inside of telephone cable that make wonderful "rigging" for Do-Nothing Machines), pegs, cocktail toothpicks with flags (and other decorations), or unit blocks

With the Children

1. Read the "Do-Nothing Machine" poem to a small group of children.
2. Discuss it with the children. Ask them, "What would your Do-Nothing Machine look like if you built one?"
3. Fill a basket with some of the materials listed above and place it on a shelf in the Block Center.
4. Explain to the children that they might want to use some of the materials when building.

"The Do-Nothing Machine" by Sharon MacDonald

The story begins—

No blueprints or plans;

A rhyming account

Of a child's two hands.

It's a story about John,
The inventor of things.
Who made a machine
From wood, nails, and strings.

He marked his machine
With letters galore.
He couldn't write words
Since he was just four.

With all kinds of tools,
John spent long hours
Reworking, remaking,
And adding tall towers.

When friends asked John,
"What does it do?"
"Nothing," he'd say,
"I'm not even through."

The Do-Nothing Machine,
John named it one day,
After months of adding
And taking away.

The fun was in building,
Not in getting through.
It was not important
What it could do.

So gather together
The best you can find.
Make a Do-Nothing Machine
From ideas in your mind.

Block Center Activity

1. Place an enlarged copy of the poem on a wall in the Block Center.
2. Put the basket of materials on a shelf.
3. The children can build their own versions of a Do-Nothing Machine and decorate their creations with the materials from the basket.

Suggestions for Assessment

Ask the children to draw pictures of their Do-Nothing Machines and put the drawings in their portfolios. Also, encourage them to write a story about their machines and place them in their portfolios.

Simple Machines

LEVEL: ADVANCED

Literacy and Language Arts Skills: To develop new vocabulary

Science Skills: To discover force, balance, and cause and effect while using simple machines such as a lever, an inclined plane, and a wheel and axle

Materials (see below)

With the Children

Note: This is a three-day activity. Before the children arrive, select the blocks and the other items listed for each day.

Day 1: The Lever
Materials
Blocks: one floorboard, one small triangle, and two unit blocks
Pictures of other simple levers
Bottle opener
Cocoa can

1. Ask the children, "Who thinks they can lift two unit blocks, stacked one on top of the other, using their pinkie finger?" (Wiggle your pinkie finger.) Let a few of the children try.
2. Tell them about a machine, called a lever, that will make lifting the blocks easier.
3. Show the children how to make a lever by using the triangle and a floorboard. Place the triangle at the midpoint of the floorboard with the floorboard resting on top. The triangle becomes a fulcrum. Balance the floorboard in place (it will look like a seesaw).

4. Place the two unit blocks on one end of the floorboard. Ask a child to press down on the other end of the board with her pinkie finger. The lever will lift the two blocks.

5. Examine and discuss all the parts of the lever to see how it works. Can the children think of other things that work like levers? Show them photographs of other levers. Pass around the cocoa can. How would they get the top off? With their fingers? What would they use to pry off the lid? What other things work like that? What about their arms?

Block Center Activity

1. Encourage the children to make and use levers in the Block Center.

Day 2: The Inclined Plane
Materials
Blocks: one floorboard, one unit block, and
    two double unit blocks
Pictures of other simple inclined planes
    (such as a playground slide)

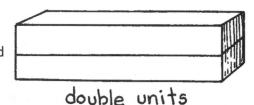

double units

1. Ask the children, "Who thinks they can use their pinkie fingers to move two double unit blocks, stacked one on top of the other, to the top of a unit block that is standing on its side?" Allow a few children to try.

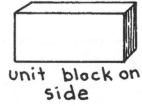

unit block on side

2. Explain that there is machine that will make this work easier. It is called an inclined plane.

3. Demonstrate an inclined plane. Prop the floor-board block on a unit block that is resting on its side. Place two double unit

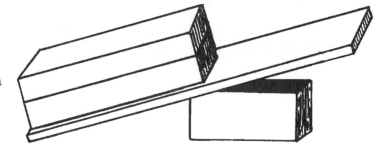

blocks at the lower end of the floorboard block. Ask a child to use her two pinkie fingers to push or pull the two double unit blocks up the inclined plane.

4. Encourage the children to examine the components of the inclined plane. Ask them if they can think of other things that work like an inclined plane. Show them photographs of inclined planes, called ramps, or point out a wheelchair ramp and a driveway. Both are ramps that lift people and cars from the ground level to another level.

Block Center Activity

1. Encourage the children to make inclined planes in the Block Center.

Day 3: The Wheel and Axle
Materials
Blocks: one floorboard, three large cylinders, and a small basket of unit blocks
Wagon or any rolling item (such as a toy car)
Pictures of other wheels and axles

1. Ask the children, "Who thinks they can move the basket of blocks from one spot to another with just a push of their pinkie finger?" (Make sure your basket of blocks is heavy enough so that it can't be moved easily.)
2. Ask the children to fill a wagon with the same blocks. Ask a child to pull the wagon across the room. Talk about why it moves so easily.
3. With the children, examine the wagon parts, especially the wheel-and-axle component. Explain that they can make a simple wheel and axle using blocks. Show them how by laying a large cylinder on the floor and placing the floorboard on the curved edge of the cylinder. Roll the floorboard over the cylinder.
4. Explain that in "long ago times," people moved heavy things by rolling them along with a cylinder and a big board. Show them. Put the basket of blocks on the floorboard with one cylinder at the front of the board and the other toward the back. Move the basket by pushing it with the board over the cylinders. Ask which is easier to use: the wagon or the rolling cylinder and board?

Block Center Activity

1. Encourage the children to use the cylinders and the floorboard that will be in the Block Center.

Suggestions for Assessment

When their behavior exhibits understanding of the skills identified above, write anecdotal records about them. For example, does a child understand cause and effect (if I do this, then that happens); does she know how simple machines are used? Ask the children to draw pictures of the machines they have used and made. The pictures will show the level of their understanding, especially when they try to explain their pictures to you or to classmates.

Lay-Down and Stand-Up Pattern Cards

LEVEL: ADVANCED

Math Skills: To learn to repeat, extend, and make patterns; to learn one-to-one correspondence

Social-Emotional Skills: To learn and practice appropriate social-group behavior

Materials
Butcher paper, 36" (90 cm) wide
Scissors
Pencil
Unit blocks
Brown crayon or marker
Clear contact paper or laminate, optional
Tape

With the Children
1. Roll out a length of 36" (90 cm) wide butcher paper.
2. Cut three strips, 36" x 8 ½" (90 cm x 21 cm).
3. Trace the unit block outlines (shown in the illustration) onto the strips.
4. Use an "AB; AB" pattern, or for older children, more complicated patterns such as "ABC; ABC" or "AABC; AABC."
5. Color the block outlines on the strips with a brown crayon or marker.
6. Laminate or cover them with clear contact paper, if desired.
7. Before the children arrive, bring a lot of blocks to the group area.
8. Make sure you have enough blocks to: (1) demonstrate each of the pattern cards with blocks and (2) ask the children to duplicate and extend the patterns on their own, as a small-group exercise.
9. Place the pattern cards on the floor.
10. Divide the class into groups of three to four children and give each group a pattern card.
11. Ask each group to find the blocks that make up the pattern on their card and place the blocks directly on top of the pattern they have. Challenge them to continue the pattern without the pattern card.
12. The children can swap cards until each group has tried each pattern.
13. On another day, before the children arrive, move lots of blocks to the whole group area again.
14. Tape the pattern cards on the wall near the floor.
15. Encourage small groups of children to build *in front of* the pattern cards rather than *on* them.

16. Ask them to build the structures on the floor so that their constructions stand up rather than lay down.

    Note: Building in front of the patterns, rather than on top of them, is a more difficult task since the children do not have the pattern beneath the blocks for reference. Seeing the pattern on the wall and duplicating it is an even harder task for children since they have to rotate the blocks in their minds from laying down to standing up to do it.

Block Center Activity

1. Place the pattern cards in the Block Center for the children to use on the floor.
2. Later, put the pattern cards on the wall.

Suggestions for Assessment

Observe the children as they work in groups. Write anecdotal records of how the child works in a group setting. As the child works with the pattern cards on the floor and on the wall, observe and write down how she makes, repeats, and extends patterns.

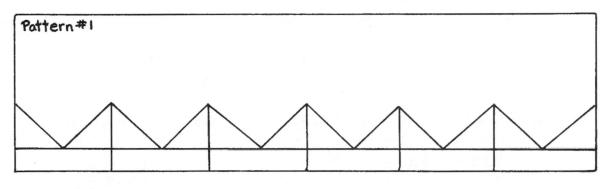

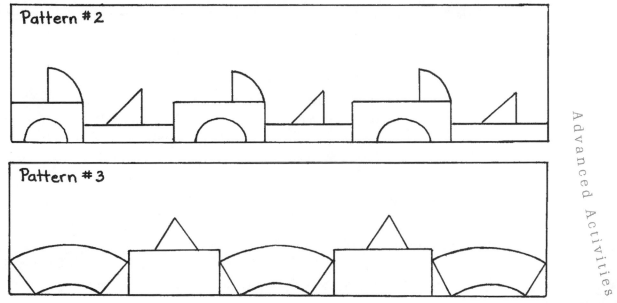

Railroad Tracks*

LEVEL: ADVANCED

Physical Development Skills: To develop hand-grasping and pincher control

Art and Math Skills: To create designs; to develop pattern recognition

Materials

36" (90 cm) long, soft-side Velcro, 1" wide; with peel-and-stick backing (found in fabric stores)

36" (90 cm) long, hook-side Velcro 1" wide; without peel-and-stick backing (found in fabric stores)

36" x 5" (90 cm x 12 cm) piece of cardboard

Scissors

Unit blocks

With the Children

1. To make a railroad track board, cut a piece of soft-side Velcro in half, lengthwise, end-to-end to make two 36" (90 cm) strips, ½" (1 cm) wide.
2. Mount both strips onto a piece of cardboard, parallel to the edge, by peeling off the peel-and-stick backing and aligning each 36" (90 cm) strip ½" (1 cm) from the edge of the 5" x 36" (12 cm x 90 cm) cardboard piece (see illustration).
3. Cut the hook-side Velcro lengthwise as described above, but cut the ½" (1 cm) strips into 3" (7 cm) lengths. These will be the cross members of the tracks (see illustration).

Block Center Activity

1. Place the railroad track board in the Block Center.
2. Put the 3" (7 cm) cross members in a basket.
3. The children assemble railroads using the crossbars.
4. They can build the train and all of the auxiliary buildings along the tracks. Note: If children are not familiar with trains and railroad tracks, cut out magazine photographs and hang them in the Block Center.

Suggestions for Assessment

Take photographs of the child assembling the tracks. (Do repeating patterns occur?) Write anecdotal records as you observe the child manipulating the Velcro pieces that make cross members along the tracks.

*   Use Railroad Tracks with the New-Block-City Floor Mat activity (pages 95-96).

①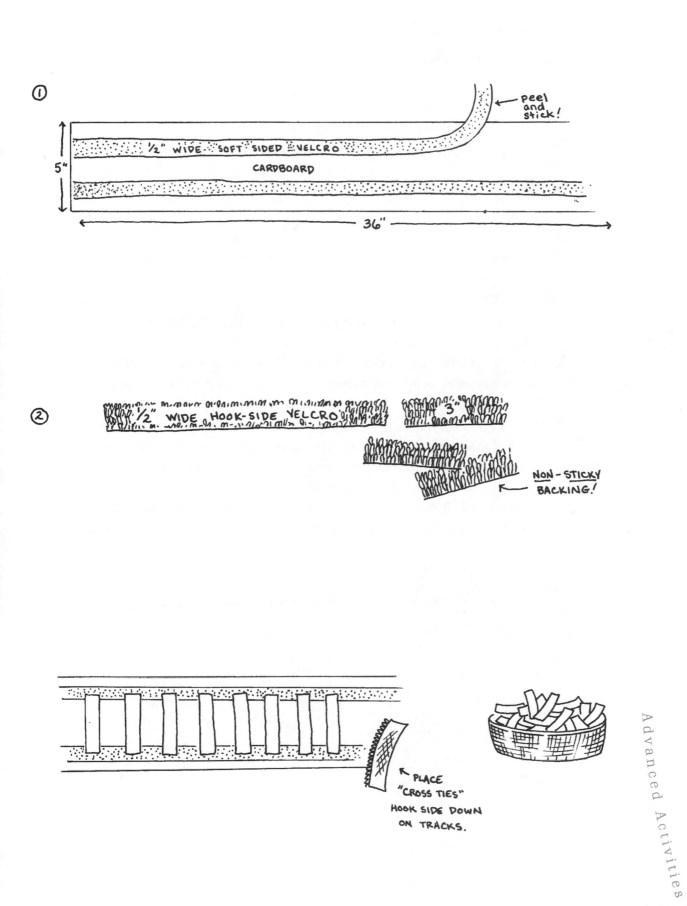

peel and stick!

½" WIDE SOFT SIDED VELCRO

CARDBOARD

5"

36"

② ½" WIDE HOOK-SIDE VELCRO   3"

NON-STICKY BACKING!

← PLACE "CROSS TIES" HOOK SIDE DOWN ON TRACKS.

Re-Creating Interior Room Designs

LEVEL: ADVANCED

Math Skills: To develop beginning mapping skills

Social-Emotional Skills: To work in small groups and learn to respect one's own work and the work of others

Materials

Basket or wagon

Assorted blocks

Photographs of the interiors of houses in different settings (task cards)

With the Children

1. Before the children arrive, place a wagon or a basket of blocks in a variety of shapes near the group area.
2. After the children arrive, display photographs of the interiors of houses. Talk about stairwells, entry halls, hallways, furniture, and other interesting objects in the photographs.
3. Divide the children into groups of four or five and put the wagon of blocks in front of them. Ask them to select (as a group) a room or object and re-create it by working together. Perhaps they will build a bedroom or a stairwell, or assign rooms or parts of a room to different groups.
4. Examine their finished work, encouraging each group to tell a story about their room, element, object, or structure.

Block Center Activity

1. Place the photographs of house interiors on a wall in the Block Center.
2. Encourage the children to build other interior rooms when they are in the Block Center.

Suggestions for Assessment

Take photographs of the children as they re-create the interior design elements or objects shown in the photographs. Put the photographs in each child's portfolio. Write anecdotal records of the children working in small groups. In the groups, describe what they are doing, who works easily with others, and who is filling leadership roles in respecting the work of others.

The "Stained-Glass" Window

LEVEL: ADVANCED

Art Skills: To create or to use designs to enhance a block construction

Social-Emotional Skills: To act out a role using props

Materials

Scissors
Tissue paper in primary colors
Wax paper
Newspaper
Liquid starch
Small container

Small paintbrush
Black marker
Basket
Tape
Unit blocks

With the Children

1. Cut tissue paper into a variety of geometric shapes (circles, squares, polygons, triangles, and rectangles) ranging from 1" to 3" (2 to 7 cm) in size.
2. Cut a strip of wax paper about 12" x 12" (30 cm x 30 cm).
3. Place newspaper over the workspace.
4. Pour liquid starch into a small container.
5. Using a small paintbrush, spread the starch over a fraction of the wax paper.
6. Place the pieces of tissue paper on the wet area. Continue applying starch and tissue until you cover the entire piece of wax paper (overlapping of the tissue paper pieces is unavoidable and, in fact, will add to the beauty of the overall design).
7. Brush more starch over the layered tissue to seal all the ends. Colors may blend a little, but this only adds to the "stained glass" effect.
8. Set the design aside to dry overnight. (Some of the paper edges may curl up overnight, but you can cut them off later.)
9. Using a black marker, draw around the outline of some of the tissue paper shapes to achieve a stained glass effect.
10. Decide on the shapes you will use for the wax paper windows. For example, make square, circular, polygon, or domed rectangle shapes.
11. Laminate the wax paper window, and then cut it into smaller windows in the shapes you desire.
12. Examples of questions to ask the children: What do people walking around outside of buildings say when they see stained glass windows? Who would wash the windows? How? Would they like washing stained glass windows more than ordinary ones? Why?

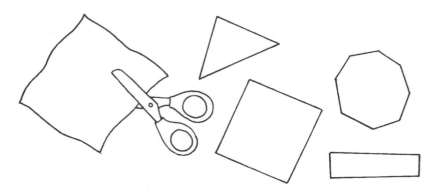

Block Center Activity

1. Place the Stained Glass windows in a basket in the Block Center, along with a tape dispenser with removable, clear plastic tape.
2. The children can decorate their structures by taping the Stained Glass Windows to their structures.

Suggestions for Assessment

If the children are able to make their own stained glass windows, save them in each child's portfolio. Photograph the stained glass windows taped on the structures, and put these photographs in the children's portfolios.

Activities Using Other Construction Materials: Beginning Activities

Build "Softly" on Quiet Sponges

LEVEL: BEGINNING

Literacy and Language Arts Skills: To develop new vocabulary

Social-Emotional Skills: To make choices

Physical Development Skills: To develop eye-hand coordination

Materials

20-25 sponges in a variety of shapes, colors, and sizes (ranging from a large car washing sponge, to kitchen sponges, to small alphabet-sponges)

Block Center Activity

1. This activity is for "soft" construction, with children using sponges as they would any other construction material. They can stack and organize them as they wish.
2. As they build, talk to them about the texture, color, and shape of each sponge. Why is the sponge soft? What would it be like to be in a sponge hole? What is in a sponge hole?

Suggestions for Assessment

Tape record the children's comments about why they use a particular sponge and where it fits in their structure. As the children work, write anecdotal records about how they used their hands and fingers; particularly, look at their ability to grasp, pick up, place, and release the sponge from their grasp without knocking down what they have built already.

The Pillow Box Tower

LEVEL: BEGINNING

Math Skills: To learn size differences (seriation)

Science skills: To discover and explore cause and effect

Materials
8-10 different size pillows

8-10 different size boxes, stuffed with newspaper and covered with contact paper
[boxes should be no larger than 18"x 18" x 18" (45 cm x 45 cm x 45 cm)]

2 large boxes

Block Center Activity
1. Place the pillows in one of the large boxes and the stuffed boxes in the other.
2. The children can use the boxes and the pillows to construct towers.
   Challenge them to see how high they can build, alternating pillows and boxes.
3. See if they can build with the pillows, putting the largest pillow on the bottom
   and the smallest pillow on the top. Ask them to do the same with the boxes.
   What happens when they put the smallest on the bottom?
4. Encourage the children to experiment by stacking the pillows and boxes in a
   corner, then in the middle of a room. Which is easier? Why?

Suggestions for Assessment
Take photographs of the children's towers. Make a tape recording of the children's discussions about why the pillows and boxes fall down. What helps them stay up? Fall down?

Blocks and Fabric

LEVEL: BEGINNING

Art Skills: To use objects creatively

Physical Development Skills: To improve the functioning of the large muscle groups of the body; to develop balance and body-in-space awareness

Materials
4' x 6' (1 m x 2 m) gauze-like fabric (or other lightweight fabric)
Basket
Brick-pattern cardboard blocks or hollow wooden blocks

Block Center Activity
1. Fold the fabric and place it in a basket.
2. Place the basket next to the brick-pattern blocks or hollow wooden blocks.
3. After the children have put up a structure, encourage them to drape the fabric around, over, or across it. Ask them to think about what it looks like.
4. There are a number of things they can make using the gauze. For example, they might build a boat shape and wave the fabric to simulate waves on the water or make a jet and wave the fabric behind to simulate the jet stream. They could make a float and use the fabric as the skirt. Then, they could stand on the float and wave at the spectators as they pass in the parade procession. If they are working with hollow wooden blocks, they can weave the fabric between the blocks.
5. Encourage the children to develop a storyline to go along with their structure. With older children, ask them to stage a play using the fabric to make different scenes.

Suggestions for Assessment
Use a tape recorder to capture the child's discussion of his structure, such as its name, function, and what it looks like to him. What does the fabric do? Would he like to make a shirt out of it? On the tape recording, remark about the child's ability to keep the structure stable and to keep himself balanced as he overlays and weaves with the fabric. Take a photograph of the child as he works. Take notes of the creative endeavors the child attempts.

Clean-Up Strips

LEVEL: BEGINNING

Math Skills: To match the blocks to their corresponding silhouettes

Social-Emotional Skills: To learn to accept personal responsibility for what you have done; to learn to put away what you have used

Materials
Roll of calculator tape 4"-5" (10 to 12 cm) wide
Black marker
Scissors
Clear contact paper or laminate, optional
Basket

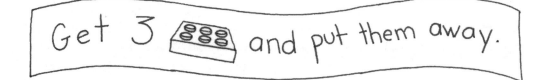

With the Children
1. Starting at the beginning of the calculator tape, write the words, "Get 4 (trace the outline of a construction piece and color it) and put them away."
2. Cut off the strip and laminate or cover it with clear contact paper (if desired). Make a number of clean-up strips. Examples of instructions to write on the strips are:
   - ✔ "Get 2 (trace the outline of the construction piece and color it) and 3 (trace a different construction piece) and put them away."
   - ✔ "Get 6 (trace the outline) and put them away."

✔ "Pick up 1 (trace the outline), pick up 2 (trace the outline), pick up 3 (trace the outline) and put them away."

3. This is a great way to make clean-up time more fun.

Block Center Activity

1. Roll up the strips like adding machine tape. Place them in a basket in the Construction Center.
2. At clean-up time, each child pulls out one strip and follows the instructions written on it.

   Note: This activity also works well with unit blocks. Draw the block silhouette on the tape, instead of the construction piece.

Suggestions for Assessment

Observe the children. Are they picking up the specified pieces? In the number requested? Write an anecdotal record about how well children recognize color, numbers, and attention to the directions. Take a photograph of the child taking responsibility for his work and putting his materials away.

Brick-Pattern Blocks with Masking Tape

LEVEL: BEGINNING

Physical Development Skills: To learn and refine eye-hand coordination; to improve visual (depth) perception

Materials

Several rolls of masking tape ¾"or 1" (2 cm or 3 cm) wide*
Basket
Children's scissors
Brick-pattern blocks or hollow wooden blocks
* Note: You will need several rolls of masking tape since using the tape is a special treat for the children.

Block Center Activity

1. Place one roll of masking tape in a basket with children's scissors (with blunt-tip blades).
2. Encourage the children to place lines of tape on the floor in any pattern.
3. When they have finished, ask them to place the blocks on the lines to cover the tape.
4. After the children have done this activity several times, they will make the tape patterns on the floor more intricate.

5. To add a variation, pair up the children. Ask one child to make a pattern on the floor with tape, while the second child covers up the tape with blocks.

6. Expand the activity by asking the children to examine their block designs on the floor. Ask them, "Who or what could live there?" Encourage children to pretend to be the person or animal that lives in the structure.

7. The conclusion to this activity is clean-up time. Encourage the children to pull up the tape, roll it into a ball, throw it away, and return the blocks to the right place. Cleaning up is more fun when you add music!

Suggestions for Assessment

Take photographs of the child cutting the masking tape and putting it down on the floor. It is quite a fine motor challenge for the young child to manipulate the tape, cut it, and put it down. Each child will show a different level of mastery. Tape record children talking about the brick patterns on the floor and their explanations of who could live there.

Build within Spaces

LEVEL: BEGINNING

Math Skills: To develop mapping skills and a knowledge of geometric shapes

Physical Development Skills: To develop body awareness

Science Skills: To begin to understand spatial awareness

Materials

Three sheets of poster board
Red masking tape or a red wide-tip marker
Yardstick
Scissors

Defining Space with Geometric Figures on Poster Board
With the Children

1. Define areas in which children can build with construction materials. Use poster board to make the geometric shapes of a circle, a triangle, and a square. Draw an 18" (45 cm) diameter circle on one of the sheets of poster board.

2. Put ½" (1 cm) wide red masking tape over the drawn line or use a red marker to draw a ½" (1 cm) wide boundary around the circle.

3. On a second sheet of poster board, draw an equilateral triangle with 21" (52 cm) sides. Using tape or a red marker, make a ½" (1 cm) wide line.

4. On the last sheet of poster board, draw a square with each side 20" (50 cm) long, then use the marker or tape around the outline of the square.

5. The children explore the three geometric shapes, and build within them.

**Defined Space on the Floor
With the Children**

1. Choose a light-traffic area in the classroom. The first week, use red tape to lay out a circle on the floor about 20" (50 cm) in diameter. The next week, make a triangle; the last week, make a square.

2. After the children have built within the three geometric shapes, place the colored tape in a basket near the chosen area. Encourage the children to use the tape to lay out the space in which they will build.

Block Center Activity

1. Place blank poster board in the area along with the tape. The children can design their own space for building.

2. The children can use whatever construction material they wish to build within the spaces they have defined with tape or colored marker. Emphasize that they must build within the space they have defined.

3. A variation on this activity would involve the children sitting *in* the space they have defined and building all around them in the "outer" space within their reach.

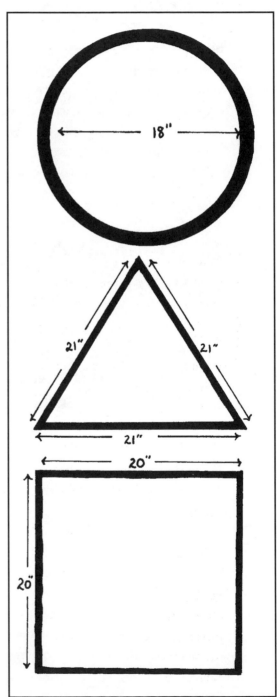

Suggestions for Assessment

Photograph the children's constructions within the geometric spaces. The photographs will reveal their level of spatial awareness and their understanding of the boundaries that confine their work. Observe the children sitting in the defined space and working in the outside space. Write anecdotal records identifying the children who are able to remain in their sitting space while they work in the outer space. Are they able to keep themselves inside the space?

Props to Use with Block Play

LEVEL: BEGINNING

Social Studies Skills: To act out roles observed in daily life, such as the work and family roles of family members and friends

Social-Emotional Skills: To learn to value and respect your own work and the work of others

Materials

Block play props (see below)

Brick-pattern blocks and hollow wooden blocks

Fire Truck(s)

Small sections of garden hose

Fire hats, paper or plastic

Steering wheel

Firefighter's jacket

Boat(s)

3' (1 m) long cardboard anchor

Cardboard paddles

Life jackets cut from paper

Sailing caps

Pet Store

Stuffed animals

Empty animal food boxes

Animal food bowls

Animal toys

Store signs

<u>Grocery Store</u>
Empty cans and boxes
Shopping baskets
Aprons
Cash register and play money
Newspaper ads
Scale

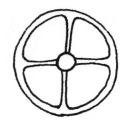

<u>"Under Construction Zone"</u>
Hard hats
Measuring tools
Toolboxes
Architectural drawing or renderings

<u>Home</u>
Pillows and books
Cooking utensils and tablecloth
Dress-up clothes, such as hats, shoes, ties, and
    purses
Baby dolls

Block Center Activity
1. Collect any of the props listed above and place them in a large basket in the Construction Center.
2. The children can build structures and use the props in play. Encourage them to act out the roles of the people in their everyday lives.

Suggestions for Assessment
Write an anecdotal record about the child's understanding of the roles of the characters he acts out with the props. Who are the people? Does he know how the people interact with him in everyday life? Also write an anecdotal record when a child shows respect for a structure built by another child, when a child works or walks around another structure, or when he asks another child if he can help her build or add on to a structure.

Intermediate Activities

PVC-Pipe Twisting

LEVEL: INTERMEDIATE

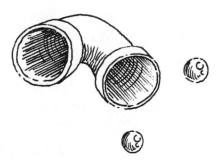

Physical Development Skills: To develop the muscles of the arm, wrist, and hands

Science Skills: To develop problem-solving techniques

Materials

PVC pipes in different lengths
PVC connectors and elbows
Large dishpan or basket
Marbles or small rubber balls, optional

Block Center Activity

1. Place the pipe pieces—the elbows, the connectors, and the lengths of pipe—in a large dishpan or basket.
   Note: If necessary, saw long pieces into short ones so they are easier to manage. Use sandpaper to smooth the pipe ends.
2. The children fit the pipes together using the connectors and elbows, making different structures and designs.
3. This is a good activity to do outside in the spring. The children can run water through the pipes to see where the connections are not tight. Indoors, use marbles or small rubber balls. The children can run them through the structures to see if the structures "work" of if they need modification.

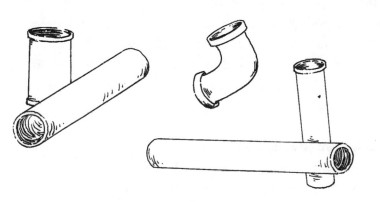

Suggestions for Assessment

Write anecdotal records of your observations of the children as they assemble and twist the pipe. Who is able to work with the materials? (If many cannot, provide simpler activities or other objects to assemble and twist.) Tape record the action; listen to the children's talk of how to put the pieces together to achieve the effects they want.

Can and Cardboard Structures

LEVEL: INTERMEDIATE

Art Skills: To exercise creative thinking skills

Math and Science Skills: To compare similar objects and methods; to develop problem-solving skills

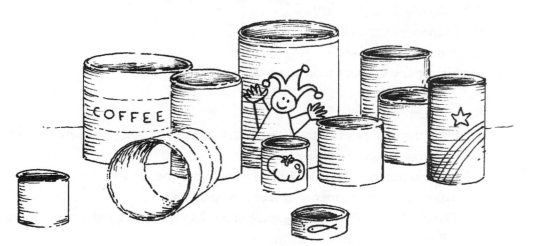

Materials

10-12 different-size cans*, thoroughly washed, and opened on both ends

Basket

Box

Several sheets of heavy cardboard in different sizes (for example, 12" x 12" (30 cm x 30 cm), 8" x 12" (20 cm x 30 cm), and 4" x 6" (10 cm x 15 cm))

* Use juice, soup, tuna, and coffee cans. Be sure to press sharp, rough edges against the sides of the can with pliers or file them smooth with a curved-back file, and then cover them with heavy duct tape.

Block Center Activity

1. Place the cans in a basket and the cardboard pieces in a box.
2. Ask the children to build two levels of the cans using the cardboard. They can build on a table or on the floor.

3. The children can set up several cans, and then place a piece of cardboard on top of the cans.

4. Encourage them to place another group of cans on top of the cardboard. What happens? How can they set a second level of cans on top of the first level with a piece of cardboard in the middle?

Suggestions for Assessment

As the children problem-solve ways to build with the cans and cardboard, listen to their discussions. Write anecdotal records of their different approaches to solve the problems they encounter and the creative solutions they suggest. As the children experiment building with the various size cans, take photographs of their structures for their individual portfolios.

Building Back-to-Back and Face-to-Face

LEVEL: INTERMEDIATE

Literacy and Language Arts Skills: To use oral language to deliver instructions and make accurate visual observations

Math Skills: To compare similarities and differences

Materials

Construction materials, such as Legos or Tinkertoys
Baskets

Block Center Activity

1. Ask two children to sit back-to-back. Ask them not to peek at the other's construction materials or what they are building.

2. Give each child a basket of identical construction materials (the same number as well as the same color).

3. Ask each child to spend some time building with the materials without looking at what the other child is building.

4. When they have finished, encourage them to compare the two structures. Talk about how they are the same and how they are different.

5. A variation is to ask one child to explain to the other how to build a structure. (Descriptive words are hard for young children to use, so it is difficult for one child to explain what he is doing!) Reverse roles.

6. Another variation is for the children to watch each other build. One child volunteers to try to copy the other. Reverse roles. Talk about how important it is for one person to lead while the other person follows. Have them examine their buildings. Are they alike or almost alike?

Suggestions for Assessment

Tape record the children as they discuss their building. Note their vocabulary, length of sentences, tonality, and voice inflection. Write anecdotal records of the children's comments about the similarities and differences of their structures.

Advanced Activities

Ramps and the Inclined Plane

LEVEL: ADVANCED

Science Skills: To develop an understanding of force and gravity; to develop an understanding of an inclined plane or a ramp

Materials
Ramp-shaped hollow wooden block
Half-square hollow wooden block
1" x 12" x 24" (2 cm x 30 cm x 60 cm) board or plywood
2 wooden cars or trucks, about 4"- 8" (10-20 cm) high
  and 6"- 12" (15-30 cm) long

With the Children
1. Introduce the ramp in a group setting. Compare the ramp block to the half-square block. Talk about how the ramp and the half square are alike and different.
2. Roll a car or truck down the ramp. Talk about what happens.
3. Introduce the word *gravity*—the force acting on the car, pulling it downward. Explain that the ramp is a simple machine called an *inclined plane,* which makes work easier.
4. Place one end of the board on the half-square and place the other end on the floor. Ask the children what you have made. It is another ramp, made with two objects.
5. Roll a car down the board. Explain again why the car rolls down the board.
6. Encourage the children to roll the car down the half-square without the board.
7. Ask them if they have ever seen a ramp or an inclined plane anywhere. Take them outside to see the slide. Point out other ramps around your facility. What is a driveway?

Block Center Activity
1. After the children have explored both the ramp and the inclined plane, return the blocks to the play area.
2. Encourage the children to roll cars and trucks down the inclined plane.

Suggestions for Assessment

Write an anecdotal record of what the child says when he rolls his car down the inclined plane. How does he explain why the car rolls so smoothly down the incline? Tape record the children's discussions as they explore the activity. Try to capture their use of the words gravity, inclined plane, and ramp.

Paper Bag Story Board

LEVEL: ADVANCED

Literacy and Language Arts Skills: To retell a story; to understand that a structure can represent an actual object or a photograph of an object

Materials

Brown paper grocery sack

Markers or crayons

Choice of storybooks: *Three Little Pigs, Three Bears, Henny Penny, The Little Red Lighthouse, Tootle,* or *Three Billy Goats Gruff*

Any construction material

With the Children

1. For younger children, draw the story scene backdrop on a brown paper grocery bag. If you choose the *Three Little Pigs*, draw the outdoor scene so the children can build the pigs' houses in front of it. If you choose the *Three Bears*, draw the indoor scene, showing the features of the house interior, so the children can build furniture and other props to put in front of the backdrop. The children also can build the story characters. Older children can draw the story scene backdrop themselves.

Block Center Activity

1. Put the construction material and the book you have chosen inside the brown paper grocery bag and place it in the Construction Center.
2. The children can dump out the construction materials and fold out the sack. They can place the bag on its side, revealing the scene backdrop that corresponds to the story.
3. The children can build in front of the backdrop (paper bag). Encourage the children to use the storybook to help them decide what to build in front of the story scene on the bag. They can depict the whole story, or segments of the story.
4. Older children can build each part of the story in sequence and put on a play for the other children. They can move the props they have built in front of the story scene as they tell the story.

Suggestions for Assessment

Use a tape recorder to capture the children's version of the story on tape. Listen for story sequence: Is the story in the right order? Are their voice infections an effort to portray the different characters? Listen to their tonality and the retelling of the story. Did they attempt and complete the whole story? How many parts did they put into the story sequence? Take a photograph to show the children's ability to represent an idea with a story scene, characters, and props.

The Circular Stage

LEVEL: ADVANCED

Literacy and Language Arts Skills: To retell a story, or an event, in four episodes; to convey an idea through an analogy, or a story, representing an idea

Materials

Two 12" (30 cm) cardboard pizza circles
Pencil
Scissors
Ruler
Markers or crayons
Clear contact paper, optional
Glue
Construction products or materials of your choice

With the Children

1. Find the center of one of the pizza circles by faintly drawing the diameter and dividing it in half.
2. Cut this pizza circle in half. Leave the other pizza circle whole (it will form the base).
3. On one of the pizza circle halves, cut a 3" (7 cm) slit from the center toward the edge. Cut another 3" (7 cm) slit on the second pizza circle half from the outside edge to the center.
4. Draw four sequential scenes that are related, such as the four seasons, four scenes from a storybook, or four overlapping patterns. More examples are four kinds of trees or the four whole numbers: 1, 2, 3, and 4 in bold, decorative print with the corresponding number of objects.
   Note: Older children can draw their own scenes.
5. Cover the scenery and base with clear contact paper, if desired.
6. Slide the two parts together and glue them to the base.

Block Center Activity

1. Place the circular stage with other construction materials in the Construction Center.
2. Encourage the children to make up or retell stories using the Circular Stage as a backdrop for their constructions.

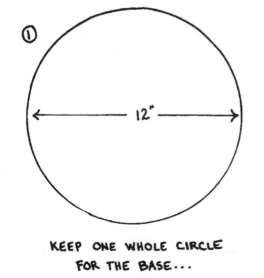

KEEP ONE WHOLE CIRCLE
FOR THE BASE...

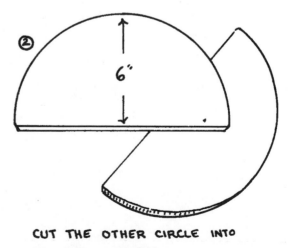

CUT THE OTHER CIRCLE INTO
TWO HALVES...

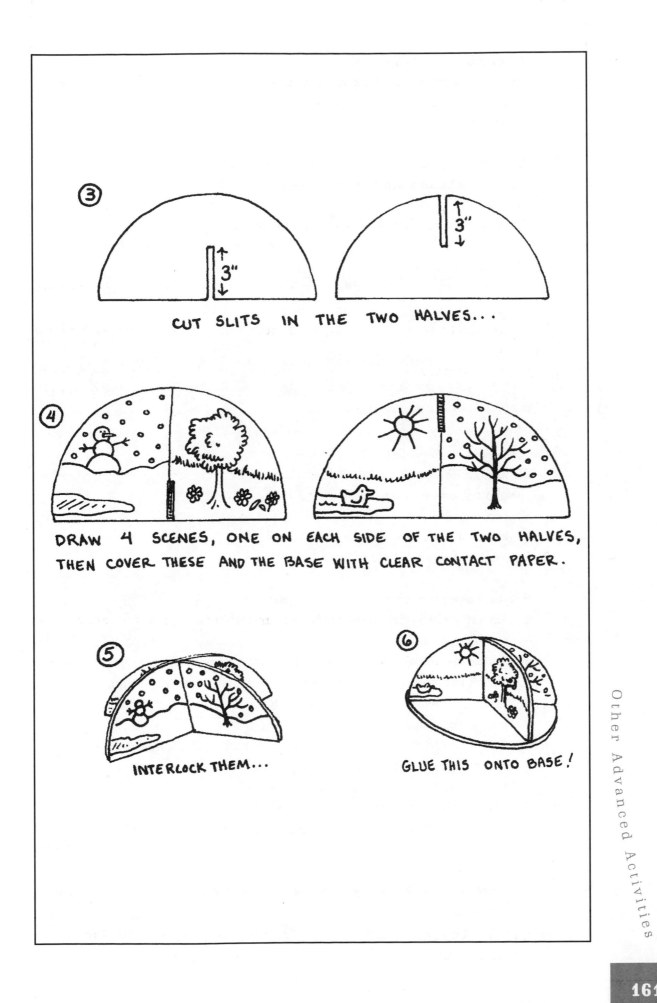

③ CUT SLITS IN THE TWO HALVES...

3"

3"

④ DRAW 4 SCENES, ONE ON EACH SIDE OF THE TWO HALVES, THEN COVER THESE AND THE BASE WITH CLEAR CONTACT PAPER.

⑤ INTERLOCK THEM...

⑥ GLUE THIS ONTO BASE!

Suggestions for Assessment

Observe the children making up and displaying their own stories. Tape record them. (The tape recording will give you valuable information about their story-making ability. It will also reveal if their stories have a beginning, middle, and an end and if they can retell a story in a reasonably accurate way, which is an important developmental milestone.) Take photographs of the children's constructions; make a brief note of what each represents to the child.

The Museum Exhibit Box

LEVEL: ADVANCED

Math Skills: To understand part-and-whole relationships

Social-Emotional Skills: To work together as a problem-solving pair or a team

Materials

A Museum Box made by the teacher
Shoeboxes, one for each pair or team
Scissors
White construction paper
Markers
Glue
Construction products or materials of your choice
4" x 6" (10 cm x 15 cm) index cards, one for each team

With the Children

1. This is an excellent activity to do after a discussion about museums.
2. Show the children an exhibit box you have made. Ask each child to select a partner or divide the children into teams of 3-4.
3. Each pair or team will brainstorm what kind of exhibit they would like to make. If you are learning about a topic or a theme, you might suggest that they relate the scene to the topic or theme.
4. Ask the children to make a museum exhibit box. (The box will display what the children decide to exhibit.) Assist them by cutting each end of the shoebox and slanting the ends toward the front or open side of the box, leaving a 2" (5 cm) lip on the front.
   Note: Some children may need a larger box than others, so the size of the boxes may vary.
5. After the teams have decided on their exhibit, ask them to design the

backdrop scene. They will draw it on white construction paper, cut it out, and glue it in place in the shoebox.

6. They can choose construction materials, such as Legos, Tinkertoys, Unifix Cubes, Bristle Blocks, Lincoln Logs, or unit blocks to build their exhibit.

7. When they are finished, ask them to write or dictate an information sheet about their exhibit on the index card. Display their Museum Exhibit Box with the index card next to it.

Suggestions for Assessment

Take photographs of the children's exhibits. Write anecdotal records recording their understanding that they made a "whole" exhibit from individual pieces of the construction materials, the shoebox, and their own ideas. Make additional notes if a child showed that he understood that all of the exhibits in the class make up a whole "museum." Also, write a record of the roles the children take on when working in a group. Who follows and who leads? Both are essential if a project is to be done; everyone has a part to play.

Block Play • Activities Using Other Construction Materials

Resource Books and Articles

Books

Church, E. (1990). *Learning Through Play: Blocks*. New York: Scholastic.

Hirsch, E. (1993). *The Block Book*. Washington, DC: National Association for the Education of Young Children (NAEYC).

MacDonald, S. (1998). *The Portfolio and Its Use: A Road Map for Assessment*. Little Rock, AK: Southern Early Childhood Association.

MacDonald, S. (1996). *Squish, Sort, Paint and Build: Over 200 Easy Learning Center Activities*. Beltsville, MD: Gryphon House.

Provenzo, E. & A. Brett. (1984). *The Complete Block Book*. New York: Syracuse University Press.

Stephens, T. (1991). *Block Adventures*. Bridgeport, CT: First Teachers Books.

Ziegler, N. & B. Larson. (1983). *Let the Kids Do It: A Manual for Self Direction Through Indirect Guidance*. Columbus, OH: Fearon.

Articles

Baker, B.R. "Development through block play." *Dimensions*, January 1989, 4-7.

"Blocks for school-age children." *Texas Child Care Quarterly*, Spring 1988, 17.

Brown, D. & L.D. Briggs. "What block play can do for children." *Texas Child Care Quarterly,* Spring 1988.

Cartwright, S. "Learning with large blocks." *Young Children,* March 1990, 45(3), 38-41.

"Hollow blocks." *Texas Child Care Quarterly,* Summer 1993, 26-31.

Karges-Bone, L. "Blocks are not (circle all): Messy, expensive, difficult." *Dimensions,* Fall 1991, 5-8.

Miller, S. "Building by design." *Early Childhood Today,* April 1999, 38.

Miller, S. & S. MacDonald. "Blocks! Blocks! Blocks!" *Early Childhood News,* 9(6).

Reifel, S. "Block construction." *Young Children,* November 1984, 61-67.

Reifel, S. "Take a closer look at block play." *Texas Child Care Quarterly,* Summer 1983, 10-14.

Weiss, K. "Bring in the blocks." *Early Childhood Today,* 12(2).

Children's Books about Blocks, Buildings, and Building with Blocks

ABC Punch-Out Blocks by Cathy Beylon

Airport by Byron Barton

Albert's Alphabet by Leslie Tryon

And So They Build by Bert Kitchen

Big Red Barn by Margaret Wise Brown

Block City by Robert Louis Stevenson

Building a House by Byron Barton

Canals Are Water Roads by Lee S. Hill

A Carpenter by Douglas Florian

Changes, Changes by Pat Hutchins

The City by Douglas Florian

Diggers and Dump Trucks by Angela Roysten

Fritz and the Beautiful Horses by Jan Brett

Have You Seen Roads? by Joanne Oppenheim

Home by Pauline Cartwright

A House Is a House for Me by Mary Ann Hoberman

The House on Maple Street by Bonnie Pryor

In a People House by Theo LeSieg (Dr. Seuss)

The Line Up Book by Marisabina Russo

The Little House: Carry Along by Virginia Lee Burton

Machines at Work by Byron Barton

My House by David Drew

My House by Lisa Desimini

My Mother Plants Strawberries by Ada Alma Flor

New Road by Gail Gibbons

The Perfectly Orderly House by Ellen Kindt McKenzie

Road Builders by B.G. Hennessy

Shapes, Shapes, Shapes by Tana Hoban

Sod Houses on the Great Plains by Glen Rounds

This Is the House That Jack Built by Pam Adams

This is the Place for Me by Joanna Cole

This Is the Way We Go To School: A Book About the Children Around the World by Edith Baer

The True Story of the Three Little Pigs by Jon Scieszko

Index